Mental Abnormality

First published in 1948, *Mental Abnormality: Facts and Theories* was written when great changes were taking place in the handling of mental disorders and in the teaching of the subject in medical schools. Knowledge of this progress reached the public in a scrappy and sometimes misleading form, and the author felt that people had as much right to know about it as about advances in the more physical side of medicine. This book gives an outline of the many and often unsuspected ways in which so called 'mental abnormality' could manifest itself, together with an account of developments both in theory and treatment at the time. Today it can be read in its historical context.

This book is a re-issue originally published in 1948. The language used and views portrayed are a reflection of its era and no offence is meant by the Publishers to any reader by this re-publication.

I0127427

Mental Abnormality

Facts and Theories

Millais Culpin

R Routledge
Taylor & Francis Group
LONDON AND NEW YORK

First published in 1948
by Hutchinson's University Library

This edition first published in 2025 by Routledge
4 Park Square, Milton Park, Abingdon, Oxon, OX14 4RN

and by Routledge
605 Third Avenue, New York, NY 10017

Routledge is an imprint of the Taylor & Francis Group, an informa business

© 1948 Millais Culpin

Publisher's Note
The publisher has gone to great lengths to ensure the quality of this reprint but points out that some imperfections in the original copies may be apparent.

Disclaimer
The publisher has made every effort to trace copyright holders and welcomes correspondence from those they have been unable to contact.

A Library of Congress record exists under LCCN: 48011243

ISBN: 978-1-032-94572-9 (hbk)
ISBN: 978-1-003-57149-0 (ebk)
ISBN: 978-1-032-94576-7 (pbk)

Book DOI 10.4324/9781003571490

MENTAL ABNORMALITY: FACTS AND THEORIES

by

MILLAIS CULPIN, M.D., F.R.C.S.

LATE PROFESSOR OF MEDICAL
INDUSTRIAL PSYCHOLOGY IN
THE UNIVERSITY OF LONDON, PAST
PRESIDENT BRITISH PSYCHO-
LOGICAL SOCIETY

HUTCHINSON'S UNIVERSITY LIBRARY
47 Princes Gate, London

New York   *Melbourne*   *Sydney*   *Cape Town*

Printed in Great Britain
at the Gainsborough Press, St. Albans,
by Fisher, Knight and Co. Ltd.

PREFACE

THE public takes for granted its right to be kept informed about advances in physical medicine, and there seems every reason why the intelligent layman should be aware of its general trends and principles, especially now that medical practice seems destined to come more and more within the purview of lay authority. This aim is capable of easy achievement for, although there are many opportunities for discussion and even controversy on clinical matters, yet the general principles of physical medicine have been stable, though not stationary, since the revolutionary discoveries of Pasteur and Lister gave a new outlook upon the cause of infections.

This achievement is not so easy in the sphere of psychological medicine—the sphere that includes not merely the insanities, but a host of other disorders that have only within the last forty years gradually come to be recognized as having important psychological factors in them. The new conceptions that Freud first opened up fifty years ago are, in the opinion of some psychiatrists, at least as revolutionary as the discoveries of the early bacteriologists. Lister's principles were vigorously opposed and such opposition to new principles is, from the scientific standpoint, right and proper if carried out according to the rules of scientific controversy, and on this occasion it was short-lived, for the principles challenged no fundamental beliefs. But Freud, like Darwin, inevitably challenged a fundamental point of view, not only in medicine, but in the lay world, which was the more fixed because it had been unquestioningly assumed rather than specifically defined. Controversy was prolonged and resembled the evolution controversy inasmuch as the new ideas only gradually became incorporated in the general scheme. Indeed, the incorporation has been so gradual that to realize its extent calls for a close survey of our current literature.

This book is an attempt at a general presentation of the psychological side of medicine and the trends of opinion in that sphere. The situation is not yet stable, for a change in fundamental outlook is a slow process; for this very reason the layman has a right to know what is happening and how his own views may need readjustment.

Such an aim was perhaps not in the mind of the planners of this series, but when the writer sat down to think how he should present the facts and theories of mental disorder he realized that it was impossible to put forth his own views as representing fully established medical opinion, but he consoles himself by the reflexion that any writer attempting the task would have to make the same admission. Fortunately most of the descriptive part of the text is unquestioned; when theories are in question alternatives will be discussed and he trusts that personal bias will be manifest when it is present.

Apart from definite mental disorder the limits of mental abnormality are indefinable. The intellectualist fallacy, that a man always knows what he is doing and why he does it, and that otherwise he is not quite sane, dies hard. It was charged against the early psychoanalysts that they dethroned reason when they declared that all of us had an unconscious which directed our aims, our likes and dislikes, even our actions, in ways of which we are unaware. Yet writers beyond number have dealt with that theme from the time of ancient Greece.

What modern psychology has done is to provide means of studying the process in actual life, and some psychologists are sanguine enough to think that the time has come when man will study himself, even in his corporate activities, as successfully as he has studied the physical world around him. The need for such study is, in these days of world upset, often expressed.

This sociological aspect is beyond the scope of this book, but there are some peculiarities of thinking or doing that involve mental processes identical with those occurring in the disorders here discussed. That is my excuse for introducing such matters as water-divining and mediumism.

Those abnormalities that eventually lead to such lack of social adaptation that for the sake of the patient or the public he has to be placed under special care, are dealt with only in outline. Their diagnosis and treatment are matters for the specialist, but the layman should be able to follow the developments that are so rapidly taking place in the subject, and I trust the brief account that I give will suffice for that purpose.

CONTENTS

8 CONTENTS

CHAPTER I

HISTORICAL RETROSPECT

PSYCHOLOGY is not a newcomer to medicine, for what we now call by that name could never be excluded from the study of the illnesses of man. Galen, the Greek physician in ancient Rome whose writings were saved for us by Arab culture, set out a theory of temperaments and gave us many words, still current, the psychological purport of which cannot be missed. They indicate a tendency to express mental or emotional states in terms of bodily function, and in this case the emotional meaning has led us to forget the original. We speak of the phlegmatic person without meaning that he suffers from any affection of the upper respiratory passages ; the sanguine is not particularly bloody-minded; and the bile of the melancholic is the same colour as ours, though the bilious influence survives to-day in the tube-train advertisement of a liver pill. Medical psychology stands out by its richness in words whose original significance has been lost in this way. Lunacy, hysteria, and hypochondria no longer call up ideas about the moon, the womb, or something under the ribs.

This richness has its historical significance. It shows an urge to postulate bodily causes for mental manifestations, and it is the survival of this urge that is responsible for the unstable situation referred to in my preface. It has persisted through the ages, not, however, without opposition, and depends upon philosophical outlook rather than knowledge or intellectual ability. The pendulum has swung repeatedly one way and another, the psychological view often appearing as vitalism or animism, and Stahl, who lived about 1690, has come down in history as "the last of the animists." His writings bear comparison with those of modern psychologists, but in his time the work of Copernicus, Galileo, Kepler, Harvey and Descartes had brought order into man's views of the universe, and it was not an unreasonable expectation that physical laws would be found governing all the processes of life. So Stahl's teaching

A*

was rejected; for two hundred years after his time medicine took no heed of psychology, and mechanistic views prevailed. A lesson as to the influence of the mechanistic view can be drawn from that episode in which Mesmer descended upon Paris in 1778 with his theories of animal magnetism. These were at first accepted by his medical contemporaries as accounting for a collection of phenomena which we know to have been psychological manifestations that should have yielded valuable results if investigated as such. Mesmer was not, in the opinion of some modern psychologists, a mere charlatan. His results did come about, but they did not arise from magnetism (as he may quite honestly have believed they did), and when that fact was demonstrated he was treated as a swindler and had to bolt from Paris. If the phenomena had no mechanistic basis they were to be regarded as non-existent or at least no concern of science or medicine. That principle—not often, perhaps, clearly enunciated—has been of far-reaching influence in the past and still exists.

The Darwinian theory, with the advance in biochemical knowledge of bodily processes that resulted from the work of physiologists in the latter half of the nineteenth century, seemed once again to hold out the promise that the living organism would yield its secrets and we should soon discover the mechanisms underlying all human activities. This view was strengthened during the controversy about the evolution of species, when it seemed necessary to the evolutionists to make science self-contained by the exclusion of all considerations that involved *aim*.[1]

It is characteristic of the medical education of those days that no hint was given to the student of the existence of the fundamental assumption that only what could be weighed or measured, seen on a plate or under a microscope, was the concern of medicine, with the necessary rider that if some phenomenon had to be admitted as existing without any of these

[1] I can remember when I first met the word "teleological" as used in that controversy. I did not know its meaning but read into it—correctly, I think—a condemnatory connotation such as we attach to witch-words like "totalitarian," whose function is to act as the bad name that hangs the dog. That psychology should deal with *aim* put it outside the world of nineteenth-century science; it was teleological.

material things being discovered then it was legitimate, even scientific, to imagine them. This imagination was the basis of "functional nervous disorders," a title given to symptoms for which no discoverable mechanical cause could be found—morbid fears, for example, or hysterical pains and paralyses. It was imagined that some structural or chemical change was responsible, but that our present methods were unable to detect it; thus the student was prevented from realizing that there was something the matter with John Smith himself and not with his muscles or nerves or glands. He was taught to examine systematically all John's physical and chemical states and reactions, but not to sit by his bedside and say, "Now, tell me about yourself," which, aided by a knowledge of mental states and reactions, is the pith of a psychological examination.

THE STATE OF CLINICAL KNOWLEDGE

That was the situation at the end of the last century, and with my present knowledge I count it an advantage to be able to look back upon the effect of the assumptions that took the place of psychological understanding in the medical curriculum. With straightforward physical disease the situation was, as a rule, adequately met, but in some cases the diagnosis of a physical disease, even if correct, was inadequate. In this connexion I recall an experience when I was a clinical assistant at out-patients and, feeling that I was very ignorant about how to handle such a common trouble as dyspepsia, asked my chief's permission to "special" the chronic dyspeptics. His consent was rather too readily given, and I studied them for months, made elaborate notes, tried various treatments, and, when toward the end of my appointment I tried to summarize my results, was obliged to admit that I had learnt nothing! A psychological examination of that case material would have revealed that it belonged to the group of what are coming to be called psycho-somatic disorders—i.e., disorders in which psychological causes act upon bodily processes and produce bodily symptoms of disease. Those patients *were* dyspeptics, but their trouble could be understood only by a psychological approach; my teachers were quite ignorant of this, though Stahl would have found it out two hundred years earlier.

The urge to find a physical cause for symptoms led to waste of surgical energy. Thus the chronic dyspeptics were often said to have dilated stomachs, and an operation was designed to short-circuit the stomach so that it should empty more quickly and recover from its dilatation ; at my hospital for quite a long time several young women each week had this improvement carried out. Movable kidneys gave further scope for ingenious surgery, but as time went on surgeons discovered that the people upon whom they did these operations had a habit of plaguing them later on with symptoms of "neurasthenia," and finally the dictum was laid down that neurasthenic patients should not be told they had dilated stomachs or movable kidneys. These complaints have now become quite out of fashion, together with dropped colons and such like, and it is freely admitted that these troubles were diagnosed generally in people who were suffering from some kind of psychoneurotic disorder which would now be investigated properly.

The relation between these supposed physical conditions and what we call psychoneuroses was twofold. Textbooks described "neurasthenia" (*neuron*, a nerve: *astheneia*, weakness) as an actual condition of nerve exhaustion for which a physical cause was postulated and sought. For a long time, as described above, displacements of organs—kidneys, stomachs, colons and so on—were accepted as a cause, and operations were designed to remedy them. On the other hand, sufferers from "nervous" symptoms tend to turn their complaints into something physical and, their nervous symptoms being regarded as unworthy of investigation, these physical complaints were taken at their face value and treated as the real disorder. It is only a matter of memory when I record that the movable kidneys at whose fixation I so often assisted were regarded by the surgeon as "diseases" standing on their own merits and calling for treatment just like any other physical trouble. A condition called "visceroptosis" (or dropping of various abdominal organs) was, however, described as a main cause of neurasthenia, and treatment of it was supposed to be directed against the neurasthenia. An extraordinary tangle!

Neurasthenia itself came later on to be described as "the rubbish heap," and when nervous symptoms were properly investigated one group after another was separated from it. Freud made the first separation in 1894 when he wrote a paper on "The Justification for detaching from Neurasthenia a particular Syndrome; the Anxiety Neurosis," but it took years for this to reach us here. There is not much left of neurasthenia now, and some psychiatrists find no use at all for the word.

There was no attempt to teach students to recognize "nervous" conditions.[1] Diagnosis was made by excluding organic disease and this was expressed in the dictum "If you can't find an organic disease you should suspect a functional nervous disorder," but having suspected it, we knew nothing about how to look for it. If my recollection is correct, we students could only picture "nervous" disorder as a more or less wilful mimicry of physical disease, with patient and physician mutually mistrustful. I recall a case from my student days that illustrates how our lack of psychological understanding left us puzzled and the patient untreated:

"A young woman was admitted to a medical ward for investigation of what appeared to be a serious disorder. She lay propped up in bed, blue in the face, short of breath, with rapid pulse and, I should think, no rise of temperature. How long she lay thus I cannot remember, nor what other physical signs were found, but the physician's diagnosis, after much thought, was a tumour somewhere in the chest, and the outlook for her looked gloomy. Then suddenly all these symptoms disappeared and she became perfectly well. As she lived in the neighbourhood and our interest was still keen, she was made an outpatient so that she could be observed for further developments. There she showed unmistakable symptoms of hysteria. When this news came back to the ward we all felt that we had been cheated by a designing woman for her own ends, and our

---

[1] I have to use "nervous" in this sense, though it is confusing inasmuch as the sense is quite different from that in which we use it to describe organic disease of nerve tissue, like infantile paralysis or locomotor ataxy. In "nervous" troubles we know nothing about any change in nerve tissue; there is nothing that can be put on a plate. In nervous disease (i.e., disease of nerve) we can generally foretell what will be found *post mortem*.

interest in the case came to an end. Years afterwards I related this story to some colleagues and mentioned the patient's name—rather an unusual one. 'Oh,' said one of them, 'I had her in my ward at ——'s Hospital, but we made the true diagnosis. She used to announce that she was going to die, so we would put the screens round her and leave her to it. Then she got tired of us and went out.' "

This physician was one of the kindest of men, but, though medical psychology had made many strides since the days when all this had happened, he had no sense of failure in regard to the treatment of this unfortunate woman. I like to think it would be different now in any teaching hospital, but I am not sure.

This example shows how we were left ignorant of the existence or importance of nervous disorders. A few cases of hysteria turned up, and the old tradition that it was due to unsatisfied sex desire was brought forth, sometimes in language of a Victorian crudity that would shock the ear of an outspoken youth or maiden of to-day. We heard nothing about "nervous breakdown," though that was common enough outside the hospital world. Our textbooks ignored it, and a student at his qualifying examination would have been bewildered if asked about it.

We had to know something about insanity, but with the assumption that it was always due to physical disease of the brain. We were taught about certification and the MacNaghten judgement, which governs the question of responsibility in insane people who commit crime. On a few visits to a mental hospital we were shown cases of advanced disorder; I do not remember any mention of psychology, and all that we were taught about it was, for certification purposes, the difference between illusions, hallucinations and delusions.

ATTITUDE OF THE PUBLIC

How did lay people regard all this? The answer is not easy, for there existed two apparently incompatible points of view. The phraseology that included nervous breakdown, nervous debility, neurasthenia, or just nerves, enabled John Smith to project upon a mechanical world the results of mental processes within himself and comfortably accept his disability as a misfortune to which he could resign himself without compunction, and sometimes his friends and relatives, and his doctor also, would take that same view.

On the other hand, there was often a dim realization that John was doing it all himself, and there was a subtle gradation of meaning in diagnostic words. We might conjugate a verb, starting with *I am highly strung*, *thou art neurasthenic*, *he is neurotic*, the last word conveying a strange mixture of pseudo-physiology and moral condemnation. "Hysteric" still carries the condemnation and to some people it implies a strong element of almost conscious malingering. Indeed, in some quarters, lay and professional, that stigma still clings to the whole subject. The young woman whose psychoneurotic illness is described above was no better off when her condition had been recognized; at that period no effective treatment was available, and the illness might still have been regarded as something she was "putting on" for purposes of her own. In those days if a hospital patient came in with a diagnosis of organic disease and was found to have a "functional nervous disorder"—a disorder for which we had neither understanding or treatment —he was got off the premises as speedily as possible.

To the public, then, as to the profession, there were two possible attitudes; either the sufferer was the innocent victim of mechanical influences, or he ought to pull himself together and stop playing the fool.

The Development of a Psychological View

Experimenters, not always medical, had been grappling with these problems since the time of Mesmer. In France his descendants carried on in obscurity, whilst in England hypnotism was taken seriously by a few people, operations having been carried out under hypnosis just before the discovery of chloroform; but it became mixed up with clairvoyance and other discredited phantasies so that it fell into disrepute, though a revival took place in Paris under Charcot in the eighteen-seventies. Professed psychologists in this country began to realize it was fallacious to regard consciousness as co-terminous with mind—that is to say, they realized that man did not always know what he was doing and why he was doing it, and was governed by instinct just like other animals. Some American investigators worked out cases of "multiple personality," and Pierre Janet in France propounded a theory (which will be discussed later) of dissociation of consciousness that brought under one formula a lot of seemingly unrelated phenomena.

But it was Freud, of Vienna, who took the great step forward of demonstrating that mental symptoms arose from buried memories of which the patient was unaware until they were revived by methods that Freud himself discovered. Using the principle of trial and error, he worked out the theory and practice of psychoanalysis, which had just become known to us by the derision directed towards it when the first World War broke out.

The Influence of the 1914–18 War

We were quite unprepared for the thousands of "nervous" disorders that became manifest during the war, and for a long time we failed to recognize their nature. High explosives produced a new disorder called shell-shock, and the medical literature of that period shows a wealth of speculation about the physical damage supposed to be done to the brain. Men suffering from shell-shock were classed as "wounded," and those who first declared it to be a psychogenic disorder were accused in Parliament and elsewhere of libelling brave soldiers, but its prevalence in all the armies, allied and hostile,[1] was such that its real nature ultimately had to be admitted. If the situation had lasted in which every man who suffered from the psychological stress of war was encouraged to regard himself as physically disabled by enemy action and then had been treated

[1] The same course of events took place in Germany. Almost the same hypotheses of physical damage were produced, and Gaupp, a German psychotherapist, coined for them the name *mytho-pathology*. These hypotheses faded out and the psychological explanation finally prevailed. In the French army there was more readiness to recognize the situation, but ideas of treatment were influenced by a belief in the efficacy of punitive methods.

as wounded, the continuation of the war might have become impossible. So, without any sounding of the Last Post, silence fell upon the mechanistic camp, the phrase "shell-shock" was buried, and in the middle of the Great War training centres were established at which already qualified men were taught enough elementary psychology to treat psychoneurotic cases, of which the shell-shockers were only a part. Considering the state of medical education before that war, one is not surprised that there was great difficulty in recognizing the nature of these cases, and many of them passed under false diagnoses. The most striking group numerically were those called "Disordered Action of the Heart," or D.A.H., which for a long time was not recognized in its true colours as a physical manifestation of a psychoneurosis.

The controversy was not ended by the recognition of the psychogenic nature of shell-shock. The medical man who had fought for a correct diagnosis of the shell-shocker now had to fight on another flank. The public attitude described a page or two back, with its possibility of two opposite views, was now manifested by both the military and the medical mind—perhaps most disastrously by the military medical. As long as shell-shock was a physical disorder all was simple; the man was the innocent victim of a mechanical injury. When the belief in physical disorder had to be given up then the opposite view presented itself and was accepted with the emotion so often associated with the certitude born of ignorance. "Shell-shock! I'd soon cure shell-shock. I'd shoot every man that had it," was not said in Parliament or Press, but it *was* said, and the psychiatrist[1] who treated these men was often painfully aware of the attitude and found himself obliged to protect them from being handled as liars and malingerers. Many of our colleagues were not yet ready to believe that although organic disease or injury was absent, yet these men *were* ill and in need of treatment. The bizarre symptoms of which they complained were thought to be fantastic inventions, and it was useless to point out that if a man wanted to invent symptoms he would invent what would have a chance of being believed; as a fact, these bizarre symp-

---

I use the name *psychiatrist*, but it was in accordance with the spirit of the time that the official designation was then *neurological specialist*.

toms often made a complete picture of typical conditions that were to be found in out-of-the-way literature (such as the writings of Pierre Janet, few of which were translated into English) but had not reached our textbooks. So how could we expect to recognize them?

Yet good came out of all this. The needs of the situation had to be met; the few men who knew the subject were able to train others in it, and from the centre at Maghull there went forth doctors who, by some means or other having become interested in the subject, found themselves in the position of pioneers of the new ideas sketched out in the next chapter. They had much to learn and because of their war-time approach were regarded as intruders, both by the psychiatrists of the old school and by the organic neurologists who had hitherto claimed all "nervous" troubles as belonging to their specialty but had failed so patently in the understanding of the psychoneuroses of war.

Thanks to the unexpected stimulus of the war, medicine had begun to emerge from the psychologically dark ages, though from this point onwards progress was slow, for all our leaders had been brought up on the mechanistic tradition.[1] Yet progress there was, and, after an intervening quarter of a century, the highest authorities in medicine are now busy planning for the systematic teaching of psychological principles to our future practitioners. Looking back on the struggle one can see it in its historical perspective as a stage that had to be passed through, and the outcome shows medicine to be in its essence based upon the principles of true science—the unprejudiced search for truth—however difficult human nature may make that search.

[1] I think it was Thomas Huxley who noted that very few scientific men who were over the age of forty when Darwin published *The Origin of Species* were able to accept the theory of evolution. Although Freud's theories were the focal point of opposition some thirty years ago, yet the reaction to the new ideas arose from the fundamental mechanistic basis of nineteenth-century medicine, and it was called forth in equal vigour by psychological theories or methods that were not psychoanalytical.

CHAPTER II

THEORIES OF MENTAL DISORDER

PSYCHOLOGICAL THEORIES OF MENTAL DISORDER

NAMES are queer things, and often carry undefined assumptions and unrecognized prejudices. Once upon a time the word "madhouse" called up a picture of a dreadful place where outcasts called madmen were confined. When systematically humane methods (first introduced in this country at the Friends' institution called "The Retreat" at York) became established, the name was changed to "Lunatic Asylum." Asylum (meaning a refuge) was a dignified word expressing the new spirit, but the stigma pursued it and in recent times another change produced the "Mental Hospital." The stigma was not to be baulked, however, and now the word *mental*, which covers all our thought processes, conscious and unconscious, has been so twisted that it is in turn used to express insanity. "He's not mental, doctor, it's his nerves," is to be heard at out-patients or in the consulting-room, and "So you think I'm mental, do you?" is often the first obstacle to the nervous patient's understanding of his condition. In my opinion the wide use of *neurosis* by my profession to indicate "nervous" troubles panders to this dodging of the truth.[1]

The words psychosis and psychoneurosis are used here to indicate the two main groups which coincide roughly, but only roughly, with the popular conceptions of "insanity" and "nerves." Both groups are equally mental. Insanity is a legal matter, and though most insane people are suffering from psychoses yet not all sufferers from this group of disorders are insane, and it is possible for the victim of a psychoneurosis

[1] It may also indicate a clinging to the older mechanistic view that they are disturbances in the physical sphere and, although some of my colleagues regard me as having a bee in my bonnet in this connexion, yet I prefer the equally well established and slightly less misleading term *psychoneurosis*. In this I have the support of my non-medical psychological colleagues, some of whom have quite strong ideas about accurate terminology in their subject.

to need compulsory institutional care and thus become legally insane without passing into the psychosis group.

A clinical distinction between the two is regarded by some of the older psychiatrists as unjustified, and cases are certainly seen in which the differential diagnosis may be very dubious. It must be noted, however, that the opponents of the distinction are generally still unfavourable to psychoanalytical theory and practice. This can be linked with the fact that Freud quite early drew the conclusion that only the psychoneuroses were accessible to psychoanalysis; thus to deny the distinction is one way of denying the fact that the psychoneuroses *are* accessible.

All this discussion leads up to the point that psychoanalytical theory and practice were built up on the results of the treatment of people suffering from psychoneuroses, and, however much or little the individual practitioner may care to admit it, all our understanding of the mental processes underlying them must be credited to psychoanalysis.

No such claim can be made for the psychoses or insanities. Many are due to demonstrable disease of brain but, as will be seen later, there is a large group in which no physical cause has been found. In these it is reasonable to look for explanations in what we already know about unconscious mental processes, and sometimes this knowledge seems to offer something useful, but the difficulty of actual exploration of those cases by psychoanalysis is great, and in most cases insurmountable.

The Foundations of Psychoanalysis

The word *psychoanalysis* has two applications and signifies both a method of treatment and a theory. The theory is built up to co-ordinate facts of observation and subsume them in a general formula, and what follows here is intended to be only sufficient for the reader to appreciate the grounds upon which the theory is based. It must not be taken as anything like a complete exposition of the subject, which would be beyond both the scope of the book and the competence of the writer.

In 1894 Freud and Breuer published the case of a young woman who suffered from various nervous symptoms of the kind that had hitherto been inexplicable. She was able to pass into a condition rather like hypnosis in which she recalled previously forgotten incidents. This process the patient described as "chimney-sweeping." The incidents turned out to be closely connected with her symptoms, which were in a way an incomplete repetition of them, and by this process she derived much benefit in the relief of the symptoms. This new departure was followed up by Freud who at first used simple methods of urging to remember, but gradually found that he could get better results by allowing the patient to ramble on and follow whatever paths of thought opened up. This was a long and tedious process to which he gave the name of "free association," and it came about that the paths of thought commonly led to forgotten incidents in which sex played a part. This led to an early assumption that forgotten sex experiences played a part in the production of hysteria, but this was shaken when the apparent memories turned out often to be imagined. Accepting this fact, Freud followed it up and found that, although actual incidents involving sex were still commonly found to be forgotten (or repressed, as he termed it), there was in addition a world of memories of a hitherto unsuspected emotional life in infancy that were associated with sex development and conformed to a general plan.

We had accepted without any emotion of curiosity the loss of memory for the early years of life that, in varying degree, occurs in all of us. Ask an adult about some event in his early life and he might reply that he was then too young to remember, oblivious of the day-to-day and even year-to-year memories that can be observed in all children, but whose gradual fading away can be watched by any observant parent. Our adult was not too young to remember; he is now too old to remember, unless we make use of Freud's discovery that the infantile memories are still present in the adult and are recoverable by his methods. It was inevitable that such a discovery should be greeted with incredulity, especially since the emotions of the infant could in analysis be expressed only in adult language. It is hard to understand that emotions can be registered without words, but only described by them.

The richness of the infant's emotional life is obvious. The eager recognition of the mothers' breast, the savage onslaught that the healthy young creature makes upon it, the angry frustration if satisfaction is hindered or denied, the appreciation of maternal warmth and protection, and very soon the return of smile for smile or of resentment for a frown. All these are plain to every fond parent and it needs but little observation to satisfy one that the modes of reaction then set up may become the fixed modes of reaction in later life. Suppose a child habitually sets up a howl when he reaches the end of his breast feed and does not thrive till it is realized that the breast milk is deficient in quantity and should be supplemented with artificial feeds; for a long time afterwards any check to an expected satisfaction might be met by an outburst of uncontrollable anger, and only by understanding and tact could the mischief be undone. A mishandling of the situation might produce an adult with a pathological inability to withstand disappointment.

There seems nothing to tax belief in such a hypothetical case. But suppose the road is travelled in the opposite direction, that the adult seeks treatment for his psychoneurosis and under analysis he works back through his unbearable experiences of frustration till he arrives at the infantile memories that lay behind them. Even such an over-simplified hypothesis is hard to accept. Yet I ask the reader to believe that such results of analysis are facts of observation and not theories. The filling in of the infantile amnesia (not really a loss of memory but an inability to recall) is the main fact, and upon it is built the theory of psychoanalysis.

It cannot be denied that the sex instinct is born in us, but in pre-Freudian days it was conventionally assumed that it played no part till its "awakening" at adolescence. Coupled with this assumption was a punitive attitude towards any manifestation of sexual interest or activity on the part of the child, whose natural curiosity about reproduction and birth was customarily met by an emotional taboo. Like all taboos this was made up of an irrational prohibition supported by the dread of an unknown penalty, and the adult who enforced it felt that its violation would lead to something terrible. If challenged as to what this something was he would not admit that he had never thought about it, but would straightway invent reasons and justifications for his attitude.

The development of the child is doubly linked with his emotional attitude to the parents. The male child finds, or should find, warmth, comfort and security in the mother, who is the first woman he ever knows. The inborn sex instinct attaches these sensations to itself and they form the skeleton upon which it develops, to be transferred later to a loved object outside the family. The father is perceived as a rival and from this situation all kinds of emotions arise, the permutations and combinations of which are endless and only to be revealed in the individual by personal analysis, though some of the results may be obvious. The youth who, in the useful old phrase, is tied to his mother's apron strings, has not passed beyond the stage of infantile attachment, and the maidens of his acquaintance may unwittingly behave as if they know he is not likely to make a good husband. If we now speculate a little we may suppose that on his side the father has his own unconscious motivations and senses a rival in the son, and any sexual interest shown by the youngster must be crushed; hence the taboo, irrational and unquestioned because unconsciously motivated.

The discovery of these emotional ideas belongs to the early period of psychoanalysis. Whether they are ever fully conscious may be debatable, but this is a suitable point at which to introduce the necessary corollary of psychoanalytical discovery —the theory of the unconscious. The idea of an active part of the mind independent of our awareness is old, but it remained a rather sterile speculation till Freud put it on an observational basis, for if the infantile memories existed in the adult and influenced his thoughts and behaviour it was necessary to think of a part of the mind in which they had their being. For this Freud took the title of *the unconscious*, and between that and the consciousness he placed a pre-conscious in which were ideas accessible to consciousness though not directly part of it. This spatial description of mind must be regarded as only a concept, a useful algebraic formula, and not as a claim that the unconscious has actual existence. After all, what is *mind* itself but a useful algebraic x that enables us to talk about thoughts and emotions. But this is metaphysics.

The unconscious is not merely a storehouse. It is throughout our lives busy in receiving and retaining impressions as well as influencing conscious mental processes. It is a useful servant in so far as it stores up knowledge, perceives connexions, makes deductions, and allows them to rise into consciousness as useful and correct judgements. The physician with "clinicial intuition" often makes a surprisingly correct diagnosis in an intricate case, whilst unable to describe the mental processes by which he has reached it, and should thank his unconscious for the work it has done for him; but his intuition could not operate without the experience that might help another physician to reach the same result by a process of conscious, perhaps laborious, observation and deduction.

The reader should have no difficulty in recognizing the same sort of intuition on the part of men who possess it in other spheres than medicine.

But it was not its useful function that led to the modern conception of the unconscious. The investigation of psychoneurotic patients provided Freud with his observations, and for a while that served as an argument to dispute the application of the theory to supposedly healthy people; indeed, the reader may make such a reservation if he feels like it, for it is chiefly because of its application to the understanding of nervous troubles that this dissertation is necessary. That application will be described in its due place, but meanwhile a reference must be made again to the part played by war experience in strengthening the theory.

Repression

The forgetting of infantile experiences cannot be regarded as due to any conscious effort to forget. Forgotten they are, and there is no simple answer to the question why they are forgotten. Throughout life, however, there is a continual forgetting which is not always a complete fading away, for many of the lost memories come to the surface during analysis. When that happens the memories generally prove to be painful or repugnant, or they have made links in the unconscious with something possessing such qualities. There is an active force holding them down, which becomes manifest during analysis as a resistance on the part of the patient to remembering them. This thrusting and holding down Freud called *repression*, and the war cases unexpectedly provided plenty of material that illustrated some of the general principles of this process.[1]

A familiar feature in the press of those days was the shell-shocked soldier who had lost his memory, and fairly often the man would be unable to recall anything about himself before some particular point in time—his arrival at a home hospital, for example. This amnesia was, however, only a gross manifestation of a very widespread phenomenon in the men who reached the hospitals for nervous cases. Losses of memory were almost invariable and the memories could be restored by methods which gradually evolved; they proved to bear a peculiar relation to the symptoms, which often symbolized in extraordinary fashion the forgotten incident; the revival of the memory was accompanied by an emotional outbreak, the "abreaction" of Freud; and the symptoms disappeared after the abreaction. In fact, the mental processes described by Freud were found in remarkable simplicity; but the sex factor, obnoxious to so many, was absent.

The methods of restoring these lost memories were all of them psychological. With experience each worker developed the method he found most effective. Some people used hypnosis, some used patient urging to remember, others took the terrifying dreams of the sufferers and made the man recall the feeling of the dream till the memory of its original cause flashed up, and, what is important, the associated emotion was re-experienced with dramatic intensity. Partly because this was an entirely new departure in medicine, partly because it was regarded as a kind of psychoanalysis,[2] then anathema to all but a few, this revival of memories met with great opposition. It would be denied that memories had been lost, or that if

[1] Freud distinguished between the deliberate effort to forget, which he called *suppression*, and the unwitting thrusting down of memories such as occurs in infancy, which he called *repression*. I find no clear dividing line and find myself using *repression* and *suppression* rather loosely.

[2] So it was. It went back to the early stage of Freud's work, when he actually used hypnosis or stimulation to make his patients remember. This was the stone age of psychoanalysis and in the war cases, with their suppression of recent emotional experiences, the return to it was quite justified.

lost they could be revived—claims to revive them being met with the charge that the operator suggested imaginary episodes to the patient or, *per contra*, that the patient, artful neurotic, made up stories to fool him. This last was the view of the late Sir William Osler, and I was present when a rather enthusiastic disciple of the new teaching gave an account of the revival of memories and liberation of the associated emotion. Sir William was a genial old soul and, with thumbs in armholes, he stood and declared, "I'm a bit of a liar myself. I could make up stories and imitate emotion in a way that would deceive my young friend over there." As a result of this opposition from our leaders the method found no place in the textbooks; even our psychiatric textbooks might contain a chapter on the war cases with no mention of this particular treatment. When the next war came it was greeted by the younger generation as a new discovery, but now instead of the purely psychological mode of attack it became a routine method to inject an anaesthetic drug into the patient and revive the memories when he was in a state of semi-unconsciousness, akin to intoxication. I doubt whether in practice this did more than shorten the process in some cases, though, as soldiers were now treated just behind the line instead of waiting till they had the luck to reach a special hospital in England, this saving of time was valuable. A more subtle advantage was that, whilst psychological methods of restoring lost memories were remote from orthodox medicine, as soon as something was injected into the patient the operation was brought within the accepted canons and became blamelessly correct; indeed, the injection is now regarded by some people as the most important part of the procedure.

When opportunity came, after the first war, to allow patients to pursue the methods of free association (too time-consuming to be used in military hospitals) the main constituents of Freud's sex motif often came up with startling clearness, bringing to the observer as much conviction as did the more accessible material of the war cases.

What is the connexion between the war cases with their brief handling and those in which a full-dress psychoanalysis, lasting many months or even years, is used? It was recognized even in the first war that many who fell victims to the war psychoneuroses had suffered from symptoms before the war. I wrote in 1919, when discussing the subject of predisposition to nervous breakdown: "Some standard is necessary and I have taken as mine the consideration whether, with my present knowledge, I would on psychological grounds have rejected the man on examination before enlistment, with his previous history, as now known, placed before me. This standard excludes from the 'predisposed' category cases in which events have shown that a certain type of man, though of average stamina, tends to react in a particular way to certain surroundings, as with the 'sensitive' men described in the last chapter; it also excludes minor degrees of lack of adaptability, such as shyness and avoidance of sports." Using that standard I found that of 192 cases 109 (56.8 per cent) should have been rejected on enlistment, and I now regard that as an underestimate. In 10 per cent of my cases I noted that the previous condition had not been made worse by the war; that is to say, the condition existing on enlistment was bad enough to send the man for treatment to a special hospital.

Although we set ourselves no standard of results, it is, I think, fair to assume that those of us then working at this specialty were satisfied if, using our comparatively superficial methods, we could restore the man to his condition before the war, and it is probable that very few of this 10 per cent received benefit from their treatment in army hospitals and that many of our patients were really candidates for psychoanalysis. Looked at in this light, the treatment we employed was satisfactory only within certain limits. In some cases we set the man on his feet and made him really fit again; in some we restored him to his earlier condition and enabled him to carry on as well as he used to; in others we failed to do that, even with the co-operation of the patient and our own best efforts; and in some the man, always unfit to be a soldier and probably never fit for very much, was returned to civil life as bad as ever.

The concept of *suppression* that played its part in the understanding of the war cases with their losses of memory, served its purpose and still does so in many cases in civil life; but for the fuller understanding of mental processes, normal or abnormal, in adult life, we must make use of the hypothesis of an unconscious as revealed by psychoanalysis.

Before we leave this subject a warning must be given about a misuse of the idea of repression, a misuse that comes down from the days when psychoanalysis was persistently misrepresented. *Repression* was twisted to mean *control* or *restraint* and it was declared that we were being told not to restrain our instincts and impulses. The sexual instinct in particular was selected, and there are probably still people who honestly believe Freud taught that the restraint of the sex impulse was the cause of nervous symptoms; they must be totally unaware that such a teaching would cut at the root of psychoanalytic treatment, which depends upon the belief in unconscious mental processes as cause of the trouble. The child, too, must not be repressed, and if Tommy wanted to poke a pencil into Jimmy's eye then Jimmy's eye should be risked for the sake of Tommy's future.

The idea of frustration of sex impulse as a cause of symptoms comes down from the ancients. Hysteria (Greek *hystera*, the womb) was supposed to arise because the unsatisfied womb moved about the body, coming into the throat and producing typical choking sensations. To drive it back the patient was given evil-tasting drugs like asafoetida and valerian, and the giving of valerian to hysterics has survived until our day, although its underlying theory is forgotten. Just a century ago Dr. Hector Gavin, denying the possibility of hysteria in men, wrote, "One might as well picture them suffering the pangs of childbirth." Since then the occurrence of hysteria among men has become a commonplace.

THE DEVELOPMENT OF THE EGO

The mind can be theoretically considered as being made up of different parts, and, once again, it must be made clear that such a spatial conception is not to be taken as the representation of anything with actual existence; we cannot get along, however, without some formula of that kind.

Consciousness and the unconscious we have dealt with. What, then, is the ego? It is that part of us that perceives, experiences emotion about, and reacts to the outside world. How much is conscious and how much unconscious we do not know; some psychologists regard it as fully conscious or even identical with consciousness but continually swayed and influenced by the unconscious. It doesn't matter very much, so long as we realize the tremendous influence upon it of our earliest experiences.

To Father Ignatius is attributed the saying, "Let me have the child to the age of five and I care not who has him afterwards," and Freud has declared that the foundation of a psychoneurosis is laid down in the first six years of life. The amnesia for our years of infancy covers this important period, and it is paradoxical that we know most about the mental life of infants from the analysis of adults, though a technique of analysis by watching and, when possible, discussing with them their behaviour when allowed to play freely with suitable materials, has allowed skilled observers to penetrate into the emotional life of infants. This has enabled us to confirm to a great extent the findings of adult analysis, though the main object is the cure of symptoms.

Actual knowledge of external events in a child's life may tell us little about the development of his ego; how he reacts to them is the key to it. A harsh parent may induce submission or rebellion, phantasies of imitation or revenge; parental discord may become involved with intuitive ideas of sex and cripple his attitude to it in later years; too little affection and he may renounce it for ever, or, going to the opposite pole, turn in adult life from one woman to another, like Don Juan, seeking something he can never define and therefore can never find; too much maternal affection and he never grows beyond it, never marries or, if he does, ruins the happiness of a healthy woman who may be lucky to get a decree of nullity before it is too late. Then there are the inborn tendencies of aggression, of pleasure in his own bodily sensations, and the frustration when they are checked which comes up so often in the analysis of adults. Training in the control of excretory doings is generally his first experience of interference with his right to do as he pleases with his own, and often becomes of great significance. The exaggerated attention to bowel function in the child that is now becoming just a little out-moded has, by its stimulation of resentment and opposition, served to produce an infinity of character defects in adult life. Sometimes constipation serves to satisfy the need for disobedience, as in the following case:

"A girl of eight, an only child, was the devoted and obedient victim of fussy and exacting parents; painfully obedient, on the assurance of an observer, but her constipation was the centre of parental concern. Circumstances necessitated her going to boarding school, where her mother delivered her to the head together with a packet of senna leaves and written instructions as to their use. The headmistress, wise to the ways of parents as well as of girls, burnt the senna leaves and by the end of term no one had asked or heard anything about the condition of the child's bowels. Nor was she noted as being unusually obedient!"

THE SUPER-EGO

Yet another conception must be explained, the super-ego. In some respects this might be regarded as identical with conscience, which I would define as the emotional recognition of principles of right and wrong, leaving out of consideration for the moment how absolute they are and whence they are derived. These principles are recognized by the owner and, if he is intelligent enough, can be defined by him; that is, they may be regarded as conscious. They are moulded, perhaps originated, by our social environment, but besides accepting the moral code of the little world in which he develops, a child may idealize a parent, identify himself with him or her, and, building up in the unconscious a picture of this parent that far transcends reality, set himself an unspecified and impossible ideal towards which he is constantly striving. This is the super-ego.

This hypothesis is found to be of use in understanding certain temperamental trends that often bring the individual into nervous difficulties. The super-ego may, however, turn out to be a defence built up against its very opposite, the harbouring of aggressive and destructive complexes.

JUNG AND ADLER

This account would not be complete without reference to Jung and Adler, who were not so long ago freely cited as offering alternative theories to Freud's. This they did, and strength was given to their position by the fact that they had both at one time been members of the original group of psychoanalysts, from which they had seceded. Except for their controversial prominence I should not mention them.

Jung did useful work on word-association tests, and his description of temperamental types—introvert and extrovert —though largely a re-statement of older views, had clinical value. From that point he went on to elaborate theories that, to me at least, do not serve the purpose of bringing observed facts into convenient formulae that can then be usefully applied to facilitate thinking. I am not competent to describe that which I do not understand, but there are people who find help from his method of approach and have benefited by contact with his genial personality. Controversy between the two "schools" has been dead for, I should say, twenty years, and the number of Jung's followers in this country is small.

Adler was entirely different. He reduced psychopathology to such simplicity that he could expound it in a single talk of an hour or so. It rested upon the *Will to Power*, which was the motive of the psychoses as well as the psychoneuroses, and served as their cause and purpose. As far as I can judge he had never really practised psychoanalysis and found his simple theory enough without it. Much of what he said was true, but it was only a part of the truth. He found considerable following among medical men and his principles undoubtedly helped them, but practising psychotherapists, though cognizant of his views and occasionally finding them applicable, rarely declared themselves as his adherents. I think his influence will not be lasting.

EXCITING CAUSES

So far I have talked as if unconscious causes arising from infancy were nearly all that mattered in the production of psychoneuroses. That would be far from the truth. In many cases, unfortunately, one can say that nervous trouble was inevitable under the ordinary stresses of life, whether because of inborn temperamental weakness or because of detrimental influences in infancy resulting in an ego that is difficult of adjustment to reality. These two latter elements we can call *predisposition*; unfavourable external conditions leading to disabling symptoms we can call *current stress*, and it should be obvious that these are likely to be inversely related. The greater the predisposition, the less current stress will be needed to produce breakdown.

ALTERNATIVE VIEWS

It is not likely that anyone concerned with the psychological aspect of the psychoneuroses would seriously question the general principles enunciated above. Some would find the psycho-analytical presentation incomplete, others might think it over-stressed. But there are plenty of my colleagues who, whilst abandoning the conception of disorder in the function of nerve tissue as a cause, still look askance at this apparent invocation of an unconscious. They look to the endocrine glands, or glands of internal secretion, as governing the emotions and being active in producing disturbances of them. These glands are the thyroid and para-thyroid in the neck, the pituitary at the base of the brain, the adrenals just above the kidneys, and the sexual secretory glands; what is called the autonomic nervous system is closely connected with them. This last is concerned with the regulation of bodily processes rather than with the functions of thinking and doing, which are the concern of the brain-cortex, the spinal cord, and the peripheral nerves. There is certainly much to be learnt about the relations of the glands, the autonomic system, and the emotions, and there is room for research as to which is the cart and which is the horse, how far emotions affect the glands and nervous system, and how far they are affected by them.

THE CONDITIONED REFLEX

There is, however, a theory that has been propounded as an alternative to psychology, though, curiously enough, it has sometimes been regarded as a psychological theory. The reader may recall Aldous Huxley's novel *Brave New World*, in which he tells, among other quaint fancies such as the laboratory cultivation of babies, about the training or "conditioning" of the hewers of wood and drawers of water so that they turn aside from all that is ordinarily pleasant and beautiful and find their satisfaction in the mean and sordid aspects of hard work, while the rest were "conditioned" for the enjoyment of everything sensuous. This was mistakenly hailed as a parody of modern psychology.

It was a parody of Pavlov's theory of conditioned reflexes, which is, in my opinion, a fantastic product of the death throes of nineteenth-century materialism. As a student I was taught how, experimenting upon dogs, Pavlov showed that the presentation of food to the animal caused a flow of saliva. Then he accustomed the animal to the ringing of a bell before the presentation and giving of the food, and soon the ringing of the bell sufficed to produce the flow. What was originally a reflex responding to the sight of food had now been conditioned to respond to a different stimulus, the ringing of a bell. He elaborated his experiments in many directions. For instance, he used the presentation of a circle as the positive stimulus, and the presentation of an ellipse as a negative— that is, no food followed the sight of the ellipse and hence the reflex was not conditioned to it. Then he gradually altered the shape of the circle to that of an ellipse and found that when it was nearly elliptical the dog behaved in a queer way, became excited and out of control and passed into a condition that he called a "neurosis." I forget how he explained this in anatomical and physiological terms, but as a dog owner I could have told him that if anyone fooled an intelligent dog in that way about such an important matter as food, the animal would resent it and grow very ill-tempered.

Here is an example from Pavlov's own book of the ease with which a reflex can be invoked to account for behaviour which the ordinary man would be content to explain in everyday language that would actually serve a useful purpose:

"The dog," [previously described as very tractable] "was

B

placed in a stand with loose loops round his legs, but so as to be quite comfortable and free to move a pace or two. Nothing more was done except to present the animal repeatedly with food, at intervals of some minutes. It stood quietly enough at first, and ate quite readily, but as time went on it became excited and struggled to get out of the stand, scratching at the floor, gnawing at the supports, and so on. This ceaseless muscular exertion was accompanied by breathlessness and continuous salivation, which persisted at every experiment for several weeks, the animal getting worse and worse until it was no longer fitted for our researches. For a long time we remained puzzled over the unusual behaviour of the animal. We tried out experimentally numerous possible interpretations, but though we had had long experience with a great number of dogs in our laboratories, we could not work out a satisfactory solution of his strange behaviour, until it occurred to us at last that it might be the expression of a special *freedom reflex* and that the dog simply could not remain quiet when it was constrained in the stand."

Why should anyone claiming to be a scientific man produce this? The answer is available and illuminating. Pavlov himself describes how he set out to find a scheme of behaviour that would exclude any psychological considerations, and he produced it by this elaboration of the conditioned reflex. This is the negation of scientific research and would be equalled if Charles Darwin had set out on his voyage in the *Beagle* determined to find some scheme that would exclude the need for a belief in special creation, and had produced his theory of evolution with that end in view.[1]

Pavlov's theory was an effort once more to make self-sufficient a mechanistic conception of the universe and exclude *aim*. In accordance with this it has been claimed that "Man's behaviour is but a series of conditioned reflexes," and in the translator's preface to an Oxford edition of Pavlov's *Conditioned Reflex* we are told that "Religion is the highest form of conditioned reflex."

[1] Darwin was, I think, actually charged with that crime, but that was in the days when any stick was good enough to beat the evolutionist with.

This is not a tilting at windmills. In the psychological treatment of the patients in the first Great War many observations of all kinds were recorded but, since that treatment was rejected in the manner described a few pages back, the mechanistic school ignored them. Now that the treatment has become part of orthodox medicine, with the added use of drugs to do what the pioneers did without them, the cases are being described again with less attention to the psychological significance of the symptoms but with elaborate and ingenious details in terms of conditioned reflexes. These help not at all in clinical understanding or treatment, but satisfy the desire for a mechanistic explanation.

It may truly be admitted that with sufficient ingenuity the whole of man's behaviour, normal and abnormal, can be described in terms of conditioned reflexes, and the late William McDougall criticized the way in which this ingenuity is perverted into an excuse to turn aside from the more difficult field of psychology considered as the study of mind:

"All that used to be called profiting by experience, or intelligent adaptation of behaviour, or the acquirement of habits, in short, all facts that used to be classed under the terms 'memory' and 'habit' we are now to regard as essentially a matter of the establishment of 'conditioned reflexes'. No wonder that in these days the young student of psychology swears by 'conditioned reflexes,' and is apt to regard the term as the key to most of the riddles of the universe, or at least as the master key of human fate. Having grasped this master principle, he feels, and in some quarters he is encouraged to feel, that he need no longer rack his brains over the traditional puzzles of psychology. For it has become clear to him that love, honour and duty, faith, hope and charity, reason, will and moral effort are merely so many names by which we denote as many varieties of 'conditioned reflex,' of somewhat complicated pattern, no doubt, but not essentially different from the scratch-reflex of the dog's hind-leg. He sees clearly that the good dog is the one whose 'conditioned reflexes' lead him to the softest spot and the best bone. Equally clearly he sees that the good man is he whose conditioned reflexes have been established by a judicious system of rewards and punishments; and that the wise man is he whose conditioned reflexes lead him to avoid pain and to pursue pleasure. *Sic itur ad astra*."[1]

Aldous Huxley and William McDougall have expressed the same criticism in very different ways.

A MATTER OF METAPHYSICS

This antithesis between the psychological and the physiological, between mind and body, does not exist in reality; it is an artificial product of the fundamental differences of approach described in Chapter II. As Sir Cyril Burt lately told us, man is not a carcass loosely coupled to a ghost. Body and mind are two aspects of one being.

As a trained medical man I know that we live and have our being through physiological processes; that the brain is a wonderful and complicated organ, derangement of which can directly affect thought and emotion and action; that besides the brain there are other parts of the nervous machine that help to govern our responses to the outside world. Over and above all this there is the man himself, who thinks and feels and acts. His thinking, feeling and action are functions of something we call mind. What mind is we do not know, but we cannot carry on life without it, nor can we discuss our doings without taking it into account. Every process of mind must have a counterpart in some process in the brain, but we do not know what the relationship is between these two. As McDougall once said, if a brain were enlarged to the size of St. Paul's Cathedral and we could walk inside it and watch what the cells were doing we should be no nearer knowing what a thought is; nor, I would add, could we tell the political opinions of its owner. There is a gulf in our knowledge which we must admit. To pretend that the gulf does not exist and that we can usefully study human behaviour by expressing it in terms of more or less hypothetical events in the brain—conditioned reflexes and the like—is a temptation that has overcome the spiritual heirs of nineteenth-century materialistic philosophy.

The brain is the instrument by which the man-as-a-whole

[1] *An Outline of Psychology*, William McDougall.

expresses himself, whatever may be his beliefs, his prejudices, his moral principles, his desires, his loves, his hates, or the muscular and intellectual dexterities he has achieved. There are many activities of his mind in the study of which our knowledge of the brain does not help us. But if that brain is injured or diseased then some of these activities are almost sure to suffer; the instrument of mind is damaged.

Here, as one brought up in the tenets of the late nineteenth century, I can appreciate the strength of an assumption then so universal that it was never stated. We could conceive of affections of the mind only as the result of disorder or disease of the instrument. The psychoneuroses were "functional nervous disorders"; disease of mind arose from disease of brain. We have now learnt that the psychoneuroses are disorders of mind—and tough work it has been to establish that. It is still somewhat heretical to think that the large group of mental disorders in which no physical cause has been found may be disorders of mind and not of its instrument.

Our Two Nervous Systems

Apart from the study of disorders that show themselves in the mental sphere, there is a growing realization of the influence of psychological factors in physical disease. I will try to explain a general principle that is becoming clear in this relationship between mind and body, and makes it easier to understand how this influence comes about.

All our voluntary physical activities depend upon the use of muscles, and there is a system of nerves, spinal cord, and brain which brings these muscles under the control of our volition; our intellectual processes and the control of muscular activities thus come together in this "voluntary" nervous system.

There are other bodily functions, digestion, circulation, respiratory exchange, temperature regulation, control of nutrition to the different parts, and a host of others that concern the inner workings of that wonderful machine, the human body, and these are, fortunately perhaps, outside our conscious control. They are regulated by another nervous system, the autonomic (i.e., self-contained), with which are linked up glands that, when the call comes from the nerves, pour forth secretions that influence bodily processes. The best illustration of this is given by the adrenal glands which, under the influence of fear or anger, send out a secretion that prepares the muscles for strenuous activity. We cannot directly influence this secretion by taking thought, any more than we can influence blushing by an effort of will; we can only do either by altering our emotional state.

The autonomic nervous system, then, can be affected by emotion. This greatly enlarges the sphere within which psychological factors can be studied as they influence bodily health, and recent years have brought within that sphere many disorders that used to be considered solely from the physiological standpoint.

Ulcers of the stomach or duodenum (the bowel next to the stomach) come into this category. Investigation of the kind of man that suffers from these troubles shows that a high proportion (about 80 per cent) are of the self-driving, highly-strung, obsessional type described in Chapter III. Hypnotic experiments have shown that suggestions of fear-producing situations can interfere with the secretions and movements of the stomach, and in these patients, with their constant state of inner tension, it is not extravagant to assume that this emotional state, acting through the autonomic nervous system, so interferes with the functions of the stomach that ulceration eventually occurs. Moreover, careful observers believe that perforation and haemorrhage, the two complications to be feared in these peptic ulcers, occur most often at times of increased emotional stress. The incidence of, and mortality from, these conditions are seriously increasing, and here we have a possible explanation, an explanation that would perhaps appeal especially to those old enough to remember the comparatively placid days that preceded the first World War.

There is a group called allergic disorders, comprising asthma, hay fever, urticaria or nettle-rash, and skin disorders like eczema, in which a very small quantity of one of a host of substances—called, when they act in this way, allergens—can produce an outbreak of the trouble. This sequence of cause and effect is undoubted, and it is probable that some people are predisposed to such reactions.

Yet there is equally no doubt as to the influence of emotional situations in precipitating an attack, and without the emotional factor the allergens may be harmless. Cases have been recorded in which skin tests showed the patient to be susceptible to the allergen—feathers, indoor dust, horse dandruff and so on—but nothing happened in spite of exposure so long as the patient's emotional life was stable. Some cases of asthma have responded to analysis, and it has turned out that the stimulus of an attack was the same that formerly produced a state of anxiety in the patient; that is, a phobia has been replaced by asthma.

A case is recorded in full detail of a patient in whom the proximity of a rose produced severe hay asthma. One day her doctor, after examining her, deliberately produced a rose from his desk and watched an attack develop. Then he showed her that the rose was artificial, and she never had another attack.

The study of asthmatic children shows them to be of a particular temperament—described by one writer as intelligent, sensitive, determined and aggressive. Even when allergens are active, the separation of some children from their parents has proved to be the surest way of arresting the attacks. Finally, very young children may produce an attack of eczema in response to emotional upsets in the mother.

Here, then, is a group of disorders, affecting the autonomic nervous system, in which emotion plays a great part in precipitating attacks, and, when we think of the ways in which unconscious mental processes can produce emotion without the main personality realizing what is happening, it is plain that research into this subject is only beginning. There is, indeed, reason to think that, even if some predisposition is present to begin with, yet unconscious processes may determine what substances should act as allergens. Lest I appear one-sided, however, I must say that certain substances—serums in some circumstances, and the poison ivy of America, for example—will produce a reaction in most people, though even then some suffer worse than others.

Progress between the two wars is shown by the handling of what was called in the first war disordered action of the heart (D.A.H.), or effort syndrome. It was then regarded as a heart condition and an official report at the end of the war took no notice of possible psychological factors, though many thousands of men were invalided out and pensioned for the disability. In this last war it was recognized that, although heart symptoms were present, they were due to anxiety working through the autonomic nervous system, the heart itself being healthy. Treatment followed that principle and as a result the invalidity sank to small figures.

Other disorders are being studied in an effort to sift out psychological factors. Among them are such varied conditions as high blood pressure, colitis, rheumatism, some skin diseases, and pulmonary tuberculosis.

There seems no answer to the question why one person should react to stress, whether due to obvious external cause or to inner psychological troubles, by developing a disorder of the digestive organs, whilst another, let us say, reacts with a respiratory trouble like asthma. We may know that one temperamental type does the one, whilst another type does the other, but must still wonder why.

CHAPTER III

ANXIETY AND OBSESSIONS

PHOBIAS

EVERY now and again a case crops up publicly in which trouble arises because of the unrecognized existence or significance of a phobia, and this lack of recognition partly comes from the assumption that a phobia (Greek *phobos*, fear) is merely excessive fear. It is not; a phobia is a pathological manifestation to be taken seriously and calling for diagnosis and treatment, and, however great a natural fear reaction may be, only confusion can result if we think to emphasize it by calling it a phobia.

Perhaps I can bring home to the reader the difference between natural fear and a phobia by reference to the very common fear of heights, which carries with it some of the qualities of a phobia. The sufferer from such a fear might, even if a non-swimmer, be able to walk comfortably along a fairly wide plank a foot or so above deep water, knowing that a fall might lead to drowning. The intellectual appreciation of such a danger to life would not stimulate his phobia and might either leave him unconcerned or stimulate enough normal fear to make him careful. Ask him to walk along the same plank over the same deep water but at the height of a hundred feet and he would shiver at the thought of it; yet the danger is the same in each case. (Many people with a phobia of heights will say, and believe, that they become giddy. The giddiness is, however, either a result of the phobia or a camouflage that enables the victim to hide the real nature of his phobia from himself and his friends; of course it may be both.)

A phobia, being a clear-cut and definable nervous symptom, with a cause often capable of solution, will serve as an excellent peg upon which to hang all sorts of lessons and deductions. So I propose to deal rather fully with the subject.

For a reason that will emerge later, the existence of a cat phobia has always been known. Shakespeare knew of it; not only knew of it but understood it rather well, and not everyone who speaks of "the harmless necessary cat" knows that the quotation is from a passage describing phobias in general; here it is:

"Some men there are love not a gaping pig;
Some that are mad if they behold a cat;
And others, when the bagpipe sings i' the nose,
Cannot contain their urine; for affection,
Mistress of passion, sways it to the mood
Of what it likes, or loathes. Now, for your answer:
As there is no firm reason to be render'd,
Why he cannot abide a gaping pig;
Why he, a harmless necessary cat;
Why he, a wauling bagpipe; but of force
Must yield to such inevitable shame
As to offend, himself being offended;
So can I give no reason, nor will I not,
More than a lodg'd hate and a certain loathing
I bear Antonio, that I follow thus
A losing suit against him."

The essential point is in the words "there is no firm reason." The phobia is an irrational fear, called into being by a specific stimulus; the cat fear by the presence of a cat, a claustrophobia by being in a closed space. Moreover, the victim knows it is irrational. If you explained to the victim of a cat phobia that the cat, even if ill-tempered, would not scratch him so long as he let it alone, he would probably say: "Yes, I know all about that, but it only makes it worse; it makes me think I am going off my head." Paradoxically, he may even say he is not afraid of a cat; all he knows is that the presence of the animal produces in him a feeling of terror. I say *terror* because that is the word often used by the patient in describing his trouble, but, since the victim of a severe phobia avoids at any cost the stimulus that produces it, it rarely happens that the opportunity occurs of observing the condition described as terror. In a mild case the sufferer may be able to control himself and carry on in spite of the feeling, but it is always distressing.[1]

[1] The definition of a phobia as an irrational fear recognized by the victim as irrational and called into being by a specific stimulus should be

Since he is aware of the irrationality of the symptom the sufferer is ashamed of it and conceals it as long as he can, both from his friends and from his doctor. Now it can be seen why we all know about the cat phobia—which, by the way, is not at all common. The claustrophobe can avoid tube-trains by saying the close atmosphere affects him; the victim of a bird phobia need not go into a chicken-run or walk across Trafalgar Square and can enter a strange house and be sure that he will not find a barnyard fowl on the hearthrug; but the cat phobia must be declared or the victim's social life becomes impossible. Hence from Shakespeare's time till now the man in the street has known about that particular manifestation, whilst the very existence of most phobias is unsuspected. When the prospect of air raids called for the planning of shelters the question was raised how many people in the general population suffered from claustrophobia, and an investigation that had been carried out on behalf of the Industrial Health Research Board supplied the answer; about six per cent suffer from claustrophobia of sufficient intensity to influence behaviour, e.g., to make one travel by bus instead of tube-train, the sexes being about equally affected. If this figure is challenged the answer is that, partly because of the urge to concealment on the part of the patient, but more because of lack of knowledge on the part of my profession, these disorders are generally unrecognized.

Recognition may be lacking even when the fear condition is actively stimulated, and some ten years ago a tragedy occurred that stressed this failure, when a man was sent to prison in a Midland city for persistently sleeping out. In prison he became noisy and apparently truculent, shouting that he "must get out of it, even if it's in a coffin." After examination by the

adhered to, but is often overlooked, and various apprehensions and false beliefs are wrongly called phobias. A cancer phobia, for example, may mean either a fear, rational or irrational, of developing it, or a false belief that one already has cancer, and neither of these conditions is a phobia like those discussed above. A fixed and irrational belief in the existence of a disease that is not present may be a delusion and more serious in its implications than any phobia. Medical entomologists are often worried by people who insist they are victims of insect infestation and refuse to accept any assurance that they are mistaken; this condition is a delusion, is impermeable to argument, and offers little scope to psychotherapy. To call it a phobia, as is often done, confuses the whole subject. *Phobia* is not *fear* writ large, nor is it an irrational belief in something unpleasant.

prison doctor he was sentenced to three days solitary confine-
ment, but when being taken to the cell he broke away from his
warders and took a header to a stone floor, so injuring himself
that he got out of prison in a coffin. Then it was discovered
that he was a claustrophobe. We were not told so, but it is
probable that his persistent sleeping out was due to the terror
that would not let him sleep within the four walls of a house.
So they sent him to prison. The matter was brought up in the
House of Commons and a medical member told his colleagues,
as one speaking with authority, that "every prisoner suffers
from claustrophobia." My sympathy is with the unfortunate
medical officer of the prison, of whom I can say: "There,
but for the grace of God, go I" and many of my colleagues, for
none of the older generation of doctors received any instruction
in these disorders. Seeing this unfortunate man excited and
noisy, any of us might have thought that three days by himself
in a cell would quiet him down, without our suspecting the
mental torment produced at the prospect.

Youths ("Bevin boys") were conscripted during the late
war for work in coal mines, and London papers reported at
least three cases in which a lad was brought up in a police court
and sentenced to punishment for refusing to go down the pit.
In one case the lad said that the thought of going down filled
him with horror; in another the secretary of the local miners'
lodge came to court and testified that the defendant was "pit
nervous" and the miners didn't want him in the pit; in a third
the lad was sent to prison but was released when he agreed to
go down if another medical board found him fit (all had been
passed as fit by medical boards). This last case was of interest
because the medical officer of the prison was known to be a
good psychologist and I have little doubt that he recognized the
true conditions as being pathological and in the nature of a
phobia; the authorities then, I imagine, allowed him to make
this face-saving arrangement with the prisoner.

The occurrence of these cases in connexion with coal
mining is significant. I have some experience of that industry
and I know that nervous disabilities generally play an important
part in sickness absence, conditions down pit being such as to
exacerbate any tendency in that direction. The depth below

ground, the darkness made visible by the safety lamp, the confined space, may be more effective in stimulating a phobia than is real danger like the ever-present risk of roof falls and even of wide-reaching explosion. The rational appreciation of danger produces rational fear, which can be controlled more easily than the irrational fear produced by a phobia.

Some years ago, at the request of his union, I examined a miner who claimed that he was disabled by miners' nystagmus. This is a disorder marked by oscillation of the eyeballs, supposed to be due to deficient illumination, and, in my experience, usually accompanied by nervous symptoms that often constitute the real disability. If the nervous miner can show oscillation he receives compensation; then if, with removal from work down pit, the oscillation disappears he is told that he is no longer suffering from nystagmus, so his compensation ceases. But his nervous symptoms persist and trouble arises because he is still incapacitated and believes the incapacity is still due to nystagmus. In this particular case phobias of moderate severity were present, but I had to tell the man I was unable to say that his symptoms were due to miners' nystagmus. He was, however, a decent fellow with a wish to do his best. I assured him that his symptoms were not an indication of physical illness and might disappear if he had the pluck to face them for a while; so he agreed to return to his work down pit. A few weeks later his wife came to me and told how he had stuck to the work for a while but at last on coming back from a shift had sat down by the fireside and cried because of his inability any longer to face the fears. I had already communicated with his own doctor, who perhaps was able to certify him as unable to work because of illness, but in the absence of any facilities it was impossible to provide treatment for him and, unless he was able to change his vocation and find work in which his nervous troubles would not interfere, the outlook for him was rather grim. On his primary trouble there is likely to be grafted a feeling of hopeless resentment and an urge to cling to compensation by fair means or foul, a decent citizen thus becoming a useless and disgruntled dependent upon society.

I have seen such results, generally from failure to recognize the real condition, though, as this case shows, such recognition may be useless when no treatment is available and when it is nobody's responsibility to help the man to suitable employment. Provision is now being made for physical disabilities to be put on record so that their effect upon fitness for work can be evaluated if necessary, but our attitude towards these other troubles is not yet satisfactory. Even in our current medical literature are to be found references to "*compensation neurosis,*" with the implied assumption that the neurosis has come into being for the purpose of obtaining compensation. This assumption must not pass without challenge.

What often happens is that the man, aware of his nervous symptoms but unable or afraid to describe them, perhaps having been rebuffed by a medical man who failed to appreciate their significance, falls back upon non-existing physical symptoms which he has learnt will be within the comprehension of his doctor. I saw one miner who was drawing compensation for an "injured back" after a fall of roof. He claimed symptoms that were perilously near malingering—aches and pains and weakness—but to my question: "Have you any other troubles?" he gave a negative. His wife was present and I asked her how he slept. Then she told how she had to wake him up because he had such terrible nightmares. When asked what they were about he answered, "It's always the same thing," and only after pressing would he admit they were about the accident, which he was trying to forget. He at first refused to talk about it, but I persuaded him to tell how his mate had been buried by the fall, how he and others had worked to remove the rubble but when my man at last got his hand on the body of his mate he realized that he was dead. His attempt to suppress the memory had resulted in most distressing symptoms and when he went down pit his clothes "wanted to go through the mangle" because he sweated from fear. Whether his fear was a true phobia is immaterial; intelligent treatment could have helped him greatly, but he received none. When I asked whether he could go down pit if his back were all right he answered shamefacedly, "It's not a nice place to go when you're frightened."

This case would to some of my colleagues appear as a

compensation neurosis; that is, one in which the aim of the symptoms is to obtain compensation, and the nature of the symptoms *of which he complained* would support that view. But behind those symptoms lay others that were the real cause of his disability and had never been elicited.

It is sometimes charged against the medical psychologist that he is credulous in accepting the patient's word about absurd symptoms, or even that the patient invents them for his benefit. So far is this from the truth that a mark of the straight-out malingerer is his suspicious attitude when questioned about nervous symptoms that, as in the case described above, may underlie feigned bodily troubles. Ask about physical symptoms that ought not to be present and the man may fall into the trap, but ask about irrational fears or other nervous symptoms and he is at once on guard against falling for a suggestion. Physical symptoms can easily be suggested and accepted, nervous symptoms practically never. I recall once being under cross-examination when counsel threw doubt upon some apparently bizarre symptoms that a plaintiff had described to me. I replied that I was familiar with such symptoms in other people, and that if a man wished to invent symptoms he would invent something more easily believed. "Then," said counsel, "you would concur with Tertullian when he said *credo quia incredible*," and I agreed that the maxim applied in such cases. In the examination of a patient the indication that nervous troubles, however absurd, are to be investigated is often met by an obvious relief of tension at the prospect of obtaining help for which he has not before dared to ask. But it is sometimes of interest to note the occasional smile of amusement when, after describing, let us say, most irrational fears and inhibitions, the patient is asked concerning a symptom that has never been present and is as absurd to him as his own symptoms are to other people.

COMPENSATION FOR NERVOUS TROUBLES

For a long time it was believed that an injury could cause damage to those anatomical structures called nerves and produce "traumatic neurasthenia." The condition was subsequently recognized as psychogenic and it was declared that recovery always took place when the matter of compensation was finally settled, though the kindly explanation might be given that it was the removal of financial uncertainty that led to recovery. This belief in recovery was, in my opinion, a hopeful deduction rather than an observation of fact. The symptoms of the two miners whose cases were just now described would have been present quite independently of compensation; indeed, in the first case compensation had never been received. Yet in both cases the man had been put in such a position that he was compelled to cling to compensation or sick pay, and a superficial observer might easily label them examples of compensation neurosis, whilst the second case corresponded to the conception of traumatic neurasthenia. In miners' nystagmus the question of compensation was the only one that ever arose; the men's unions devoted their energy to obtaining it and, I have reason to believe, my views that the disability is largely nervous and not due to a physical disease are regarded in some quarters as dictated by hostility to the miner. Unfortunately there is reason in that attitude, for as long as the trouble is regarded as physical then the mechanistic-minded doctor is ready to grant the need for compensation, but he will—and does—express strong disapproval when I maintain that the existence of a severe phobia is as disabling as a physical disease. "If a miner has phobias," said one to me, "the proper thing is to stop his compensation and make him go down pit," and that point of view may have been responsible for the episode of the three Bevin boys, though I doubt whether in those cases the existence of the phobias was even suspected. Unfortunately the matter of compensation is regarded by both sides as the beginning and end of the difficulty, and as long as that attitude remains no solution is possible. (I learn that in Scotland the number of certifications of nystagmus is diminishing, probably because ordinary sick benefit has been made equal to compensation, but that leaves the real situation practically unchanged.) It was once suggested that "miners' neurosis" should be made subject to compensation, but I was opposed to that. To keep the emphasis upon compensation would be recognized as absurd in the case of physical injury or disease; treatment and rehabilitation stand out as the prime necessities, whilst financial aid and reassurance are only adjuvants. It may be a long time before psychotherapy is available whenever it is needed, but at least the nervous victim should be given some other choice than between, on the one hand, struggling along as best he can with neither understanding nor treatment, and, on the other, becoming a hopeless dependent upon compensation. Meanwhile I take my stand against the idea, so glibly expressed in the phrase *compensation neurosis*, that the neurosis is produced, or at least maintained, by the desire for compensation. There are rogues who malinger either physical or nervous disease, but their existence does not lessen our obligation to the honest man.

THE CAUSE OF PHOBIAS

The phobia, like most other striking nervous symptoms, rarely stands alone. That is to say, it is only part of a general psychoneurosis, though because of its definite character it often appears to be an isolated manifestation. If a man suffers from a phobia he is often surprised, on consulting a doctor, to find that other symptoms which he had thought to be unrelated are part of the same picture. Yet, because of its definite nature it may be possible to elucidate its specific cause and remove it whilst the general psychoneurosis remains *in statu quo*. The first case of such an elucidation to be reported in the medical literature of England was described by the late Dr. W. H. R. Rivers in the *Lancet*, in 1917, and is rightly regarded as classical. The patient had, among other symptoms, suffered from a severe claustrophobia, and Dr. Rivers was fortunate enough to recover, by means of a dream, a memory of his having been accidentally shut in a dark passage, when a child, with a big dog that terrified him. With the revival of this memory the phobia disappeared, and, to silence objectors who might, and did, to my knowledge, declare that he "suggested" the incident to the man, Dr. Rivers took the trouble to interview his parents, who confirmed the truth of the story.

Another early case was that recorded by the late Dr. C. S. Myers, in which the patient, an ex-service man, was unable to travel on top of a tram with an overhead trolley-wire, because the noise of the wire terrified him. Using suitable technique, Dr. Myers was able to recall a specific incident of warfare when the man had been terrified by the whistling of shells; the noise of the wire had called up the terror but not the memory of the incident and the revival once again was curative of the particular symptom. It must be stressed that it is not the explanation that helps; if Myers had rightly guessed what the noise signified and explained it, the patient might well have replied: "Yes, that's very interesting, but it doesn't help." The memory must be actually recalled and felt as real by the subject.

These cases, though useful as the illustration of a principle, are misleading inasmuch as few phobias prove to be so simple. The origin of most is far more complex and calls for lengthy psychoanalysis, the phobia disappearing only when the deep foundations of the whole psychoneurosis are laid bare. It may perhaps symbolize, for example, fear of the patient's own infantile aggressiveness and have little or no relation to any memory of material events. I know of one lady who, among other and more disabling symptoms, had one strange phobia. She was no mean bridge player, but when dummy's hand went down and she saw the possibility of a grand slam, the terror came upon her. In the course of analysis of her own aggressiveness she suddenly realized with considerable emotion the significance of the phobia, which a bridge player can best understand, for in playing for a slam one's opponents must never be allowed a "look in"; they are under one's thumb and must be kept there. The terror was the expression of fear of this relentlessness, or rather of the primitive aggressiveness that it symbolized; no actual memory of any event was concerned. I recall one war-time case in which a cat phobia was readily solved by the revival of the memory of a cat making herself comfortable on the face of a child in its cot; on the other hand, the lengthy analysis of a cat phobia has been described in which all sorts of sex fears and fantasies had become associated with the idea of the cat—largely because that animal "walks by itself," and seems to live in a world all its own. The summation of these fears produced a phobia that was a serious limitation to the patient's activities.

Between these extremes are found cases in which an actual

incident has been the genesis of the phobia but has attracted to itself subsequent, or even precedent, fears and anxieties; the discovery of the repressed memory then becomes only the starting-point of a deeper analysis.

OBSESSIONAL SYMPTOMS

The word *obsession* (from *obsidere*, to besiege) has come to be applied to certain troubles because of the patient's feeling that, hostile to his real self, they relentlessly thrust themselves upon him and have to be resisted. It is often wrongly used to indicate a delusion or other false idea that is *not* resisted. Obsessions are closely connected with the temperament of the patient and a few words about that are necessary.

Volumes have been written about temperament, which might be defined as the inborn tendency to react in a particular way to external stimuli. Differences can be observed early in infancy; one child is alert, quick to react, and spends little time in taking thought; another is slower to respond, observes rather than acts, and soon shows a contemplative way of life. Both are equally healthy and if the world goes well with them neither should be afflicted by nervous symptoms. But if something goes ill then their initial make-up will have a share in determining what kind of nervousness will develop.

These two types have been recognized for ages. One might call them the tough-minded and the tender-minded; current terms are extrovert and introvert, but once again we must beware of pigeon-holes and, whilst recognizing the usefulness of the classification, be prepared for anomalies, overlapping, and the danger of hasty judgements.

The extrovert, if he falls a victim to a psychoneurosis, will tend to stress the physical nature of his symptom and have difficulty in admitting its mental nature. The introvert, already prone to self-examination, may from the start recognize that his symptom arises within his own mind. This is clearly seen in those twitching movements called tics, which we have all noticed at some time or other. The extrovert will regard them as due to some physical cause for which he is in no way responsible; the introvert often says, "I know I am doing this, but I can't stop it," or even, "I know I can stop this, but it costs such a terrible effort that I let it go on again."

The extrovert is sociable, lacking in self-consciousness, and readily accepts the views of the world he lives in. Free from the urge to self-examination, he succeeds when decision and action are needed, and my fellow psychologists would probably agree that only an extrovert could take the stress of two Great Wars and then have the physical and mental energy for an electoral campaign as our great leader did.

The introvert is shy, has to feel his way, is reflective and inclined to speculative thought, may be over-scrupulous and prone to drive himself hard, and is emotionally restrained or even inhibited. He often finds satisfaction in painstaking and original work, many successful scientific men belonging to the type.

If these introvert qualities become exaggerated they pass into a group of symptoms called obsessional, and it is often hard to judge whether we should call a man an extreme introvert or say he has an obsessional make-up. Let me draw an imaginary picture of such a case:

"A. B. says he is highly strung. Sometimes feels he is under observation when he knows he is not. Checks his work very carefully; would hate to be found out in a mistake; only feels at home with people he knows very well. Never very good at games. Enjoys country walks alone. Has to meet important people and is always very nervous beforehand, but does well when he is called upon. If he has a task to do he must put out all his energy even if there is no hurry. Has a few superstitious ideas that he knows are foolish—e.g., counts the carriages in a train and says, 'If it's an odd number I shall be lucky.' Never mixed readily with the opposite sex but is happily married."

A useful criterion is whether his efficiency or happiness is interfered with by his make-up, and it is almost the rule to find that the man is highly esteemed for his reliability and devotion to duty. If, however, some frustration occurred, especially in the personal relationships of his work, he might take it so much to heart that a breakdown would follow.

It is noteworthy that such a person will often, on questioning, tell of a parent with high principles whom he esteems very greatly. From the psychoanalytical point of view he may be said to have taken into himself the parental image and exaggerated it, so that he has set up an unspecified ideal towards which he must be for ever striving—a super-ego. Yet a brother, brought up apparently in a similar manner, may be a thorough extrovert. Whether this is due to some accidental difference in the handling of the two infants in early life, or to original temperamental dissimilarity, is a debatable question. I incline to the latter view.

I once met a strange confirmation of this "father image" in an African native who had received a European education. In an interview with him I discovered the obsessional make-up and put it to him that he had a high-principled parent whom he greatly esteemed. To this he replied with a delightful description of his father as a tribal chief who had impressed upon the growing boy the traditions and moral principles of his people, principles which, he assured me, he valued as highly as anything he had ever learnt from his white teachers.

It is necessary to keep to the meaning of "obsession," which is often loosely used to indicate various mental processes. The obsession is recognized by the patient at its true value; rising into his consciousness, it urges him to say or do or think something, or to experience some emotion, but though he feels the compulsion he is aware of its unfitness for the circumstances. Moreover it never takes full possession of his consciousness and he has always other conscious tendencies to oppose it.

We meet with doubts, especially in intellectual activities; in mild cases the man is unable to "make up his mind"; in talking about his future he will, if allowed, wander round and about the subject, presenting foolish objections to every proposed course of action, and if advised to take a certain course he may agree to do so, but at the next interview will tell of various emotions and ideas which have prevented him from carrying out the intention. One patient, when told to join an educational class, asked, "Can you tell me, sir, why I have been wanting to join the class for five weeks and haven't been able to bring myself to do it?" The question is quite typical of the attitude. The doubts that assail these people seem ridiculous, but they are very real to the sufferers; one man cannot post a letter without returning to make sure that he has not dropped it on the ground instead of putting it in the letter-box, another must always open a letter he has sealed in order to make sure that he has said nothing absurd in it. Many of us have these tendencies at times, but the obsessional must give way to them or suffer anxiety; the same comparison applies to the apparently trivial obsessions that beset him—to count the panels of a fence, to look up dark entries, or to read posters—he must do it or suffer.

There is no end to the varieties of obsession; they include exacerbations of foibles that are well within ordinary limits. About one person in four here in London pays some attention as to whether he walks on or between the cracks of the pavement, and may recognize that he does it more constantly if he happens to be worried; but he need not do it and it costs him no effort to stop. If, however, he *must* do it or have an uncomfortable feeling as of something left undone then he is becoming obsessional. It is related of Dr. Johnson that he was seen to touch each post as he walked down a court and that, omitting one, he retraced his steps to complete the ritual. I link this with the other peculiarity that he could not bear the mention of death; they were both obsessional symptoms.

We all at some time or other find a tune running through our heads and cannot banish it; that is quite ordinary. But suppose that instead of a tune it is an unpleasant or blasphemous phrase that won't keep out; then we may justifiably seek treatment if it worries us enough.

Here are some symptoms, as described by the patients themselves, that illustrate their infinite variety.

"I had to give up playing chess because I had an obsession to arrange everyone, even in the street, in accordance with the bishop's or knight's move."

"I dissect my actions and then dissect the dissections. It's a vicious circle till I nearly go mad. I try but can't stop."

"If I am typing a letter and make one mistake I never correct it. I must tear it up and start again."

"If I see a man on a ladder I am seized with the fear that if I think of him falling perhaps I shall make him fall."

"I *know* I have done something but I *feel* that I haven't. I have walked back to the office to try the door, though I *know* I've locked it."

One obsessional condition that, according to some observers, has increased of late years, is loss of the sense of reality, when the outer world seems unreal, or depersonalization, when the self seems unreal. I was once told by a working man who suffered from this depersonalization, "I'm sitting on this chair but I feel there is nothing inside my clothes, and I don't know my head is there till I put my cap on it." It is very distressing, and often the patient finds himself unable to describe it so that his friends or his doctor can understand it. The symptom can occur apart from the obsessional make-up, but there is no doubt that it can often be elucidated by psychoanalysis and proves then to be obsessional.

In all the varied manifestations of this kind it is most useful for the victim to tell of his trouble and learn that it is not, as he often fears, a sign of insanity.

There is another important reason for the obsessional to discuss his symptoms. One frequently reads the report of an inquest upon someone who had no material worries, financial or other, who was highly regarded by his friends and business associates for his conscientiousness and devotion to duty, but who had overworked himself excessively and then, to the surprise of everybody, had committed suicide. Almost invariably the tragedy is ascribed to the over-work, but the reader will recognize the description of the obsessional worrier with the urge towards an impossible ideal. The over-work was not a cause but a symptom, and no one has any idea of what other unrevealed symptoms may have been present. There is good reason to think that in these cases a timely discussion with an informed listener would have averted the disaster. Such cases have to be distinguished from those in which a depressed patient has been obviously and excessively brooding over real or unreal troubles; they are generally cases of melancholia, a condition calling for quite different handling.

As to the treatment of these troubles, in those of lesser degree much can be done by discussion and encouragement and the adjustment of material conditions; anxiety symptoms are often conjoined and can be treated on psychoanalytical principles. The obsessional make-up itself is accessible to analysis, but that is likely to be prolonged and difficult. In severe and disabling cases the new operation of leucotomy may prove to be justifiable and is now on trial.

STAMMERS, LEFTHANDEDNESS, AND CRAMPS

There used to be a distinction between a stutter and a stammer, the former consisting in the interpolation of adventitious sounds, the latter in difficulty with initials or words, one being ascribed to interference with articulation, the other to a disturbance in the breathing mechanism. This distinction is useful when methods of treatment by encouragement and re-education are employed, but if we regard the disorder psychologically as something the patient himself is doing, then the *why* becomes more important than the *how*.

In the first World War stammers were very common among the nervous results of war stress. In many cases immediate cure of the stammer followed the pouring out of emotional experiences at one interview; in others a fuller exploration was necessary and the stammer, instead of representing a single primary emotion, was found to carry the symbolism of many repressed emotional memories. In such patients each stereotyped grimace or tic might bear its own meaning, and disappeared when the meaning became conscious. In one N.C.O. a spasm of the lower jaw represented the putting on of a gas mask, a boring movement of the head was a repetition of attempts to crawl from beneath a collapsing kite balloon whilst a hostile airman sought to set fire to it, a pulling at the lapel of the patient's coat signified the agitated tugging at his whistle in emergencies, and several difficult letters "stood for" words expressing ideas of great emotional value. Each symptom could be used as a means of reviving the memory directly concerned; if directed to repeat continuously an initial letter that troubled him, the man would become emotional, and then, with a little stimulus, could recall the word for which it stood and the whole story associated with it. The letter S, for example, stood for "Steady," which referred to an occasion when he tried to restrain his men from bolting when they were being killed all around him.

The material was enough to establish that stammering is an expression of emotion arising from an unconscious motivation. Here fiction has been in advance of medicine; the actor or story-teller will employ a stammer to represent terror or embarrassment, thus demonstrating that its emotional significance is understood. The mere observation of stammers that arose apart from war stress—whether dating from childhood or acquired in later life—may render plain the kind of emotion they express; expostulation, fear, embarrassment, doubt, even the checking of childish sobs, can all be detected in the stammers of adults. I once knew a gentleman whose stammer originated on the only occasion in his life when he became intoxicated; he had been treated unsuccessfully by re-education and hypnotic suggestion without this fact being elicited, but later on a little exploration revealed that during the convivial process there had been an underlying dread of "What would Father say?" His relations with his father had always been satisfactory, but this dread, grafted upon some infantile complex, was sufficient to start and maintain the stammer, which disappeared when this understanding was reached. Sometimes the analysis of an adult stammer shows it to be loaded with symbolic meanings just as was that of the N.C.O. described above.

Observers have noted a curious obstinacy in the stammerer. He may be brought to speak clearly in an ordinary voice— whether by re-education or psychoanalysis—but refuses to use that voice, declaring perhaps that it is "not himself" and therefore he will not use it. One who had been re-educated by first singing and then bringing his voice to ordinary speech, used it for a time and then deliberately returned to the stammer, declaring that he would not sing any longer. Such an attitude finds its counterpart in an actor who stammered badly *except when he was on the stage*! All this suggests an affinity with the obstinacy of the lefthander, which is shortly to be described.

Stammer and lefthandedness tend to occur in the same family. If a lefthanded child is compelled to become righthanded he often develops a stammer, and for this phenomenon there is a simple anatomical explanation. Muscular movements of the righthand side of the body are controlled by the lefthand side of the brain; in righthanded people speech is also controlled by the lefthand side of the brain. In lefthanders this is reversed and the righthand side of the brain that controls the master hand now controls speech. If the left hand is the master to begin with, and the mastery is transferred to the right hand, then it is assumed that speech control must likewise be transferred to the other side of the brain. Because of this transfer, control is thrown out of gear and stammer results. A simple theory, but it demands a cause of stammer entirely different from the psychological causes described above. Moreover, stammer never results in the many righthanders who lose the right arm and are compelled to place the control of all manual activity on the other side of the brain, even though the loss so often occurs in adult life when the anatomical relationships should have become so much more fixed and the change-over so much more difficult.

In an effort to solve this contradiction let us look at lefthandedness. My friend, Mr. W. S. Inman, has paid attention to the subject and here are some of his views:

"Independence is characteristic of the lefthander, and seems to be related to the development of the abnormality. Whether a lefthander (and it may be noted that lefthandedness is more common among boys than girls) was born with a capacity for complete ambidexterity and tenaciously clings to such lefthanded activities as have survived parental pressure, resenting strongly meanwhile the interference with his personal desire to do as he likes with his own hands, or whether he has actually adopted lefthandedness as a sign of his desire to be different from the authoritative parent, the fact remains that the lefthanded child is almost invariably more critical and self-sufficient than his squinting and stammering relatives. The latter certainly are often very obstinate and obstructive, but there is an absence of effective reaction in their attitudes. In opposing authority, the lefthander as a rule maintains a mental poise which generally, though not always, saves him from suffering too much in his own person. In two cases of lefthanded sons of medical men the attempt to abolish the lefthandedness was followed by a stammer. One of these patients, when asked a few years later what his emotional state had been at the time of the attempt, answered: 'I resented it, and felt it was an insult.' "

Any observer can confirm or refute this independence of the lefthander. He rarely "goes baldheaded" at a difficulty, but rather follows his own road calmly and obstinately. He has a sense of justice, for himself and others, and likes to carry through his plans himself. The writer of the story of the killing of the tyrant Eglon (Judges iii, 15), surely had these characteristics in mind when he wrote of "Ehud . . . a man lefthanded," as if to say "That's the sort of fellow he was." The emphasis of the story is upon his deliberate planning, his single-minded determination, his independence of all help, even to the making of his own dagger; and the result is a picture of the lefthander *in excelsis*.

Let us now imagine Inman's lefthanded child, whether he clings to innate lefthanded activities or has developed them as a symbol of independence. Compelled by the all-powerful father to renounce his right to do as he will with his own hands, he is broken in spirit and expresses defeat and resentment in a stammer. Look at the other side and ask why parents, and teachers too, used to deny to the lefthander the right to stay as he was. They probably could produce material reasons and argue that the change was for his own good, but at bottom was the feeling that here was a rebel who would not conform to the custom of the herd and must be broken. So they broke him. It is satisfactory that most educationalists to-day give a child the right to be lefthanded.

Occupational Cramps

These are disorders that interfere with activities generally, but not always, belonging to a specific occupation. Such are writers', telegraphists', violinists', cigarette-makers' and other cramps, some forty having been described at one time or another.

At first sight they appear as disorders of muscle or nerve, and for a long time they were thus regarded, treatment being by massage, electricity and other local measures. The first to be psychologically studied was telegraphists' cramp, which showed itself in the use of the Morse key. Anomalous symptoms were soon discovered, which indicated without doubt a strong mental element. For the following example I am indebted to a personal communication from my colleague Dr. May Smith:

"A man disabled by cramp was being examined to find out what pressure he used on the Morse key. An ordinary key was attached to an instrument for recording pressure, and, the apparatus being shown to him, he was invited to use the key as if telegraphing. This he did quite easily, and he was then asked to send off a message. This he also did easily and successfully. To the remark 'But I thought you had cramp,' he straightway answered, 'Yes, so I have, but this isn't sending a telegram.'"

This was inconsistent with any physical disorder. When he knew the key was attached to a pressure-meter the man could use it without trouble; but if he knew it was attached to a wire, with someone noting the dots and dashes at the other end, then his muscles were thrown into cramp and sending became impossible.

He was like a stammerer who can read aloud to himself quite happily but stammers when he knows someone is listening. Another analogy with stammer was difficulty with particular letters; one cramp subject tripped at C, K, and Q, the hard sound plainly meaning something to him. Besides this, many cramp subjects suffered from severe psychoneurotic troubles in addition to the conspicuous symptom, which thus fell into place as part of a general picture. Finally it became clear that telegraphists' cramp was something the man was doing and not an affection of muscle or nerve; it was no use asking him *why* he was doing it, the answer to that question could only be discovered by psychoanalysis, as in the N.C.O. stammerer described above.

Writers' cramp, when investigated in the same way, conformed to the same type. Some cramp subjects, for instance, only suffer when under observation. My own experience is that it occurs fairly often in people whose occupation does not involve excessive writing.

I have seen it in a market gardener and a hotel cellarman, and also in people of "no occupation." Enough patients have subjected themselves to analytical treatment to confirm that unconscious mental processes lie behind the symptoms. It is a stammer of the hand.

These views are not yet fully incorporated in medical teaching; there are medical men who still find it difficult to accept them and there are patients who prefer explanations in terms of rheumatism or neuritis rather than be persuaded that their trouble arises within themselves.

Degrees of Nervous Disability

The psychological theories laid down in the previous chapter have had little reference to external influences in provoking or exacerbating nervous trouble. While it is true that the foundations of a psychoneurosis are laid in the first few years of life, yet it is by no means inevitable that it should become disabling in later years. In my industrial researches it was forced upon me that a distinction must be drawn between nervous symptoms and nervous disability, for I discovered that some 30 per cent of the working population suffered from an occasional symptom—perhaps a mild phobia—that did not interfere with happiness or efficiency, that another 25 per cent had symptoms that in some degree did so interfere, though they carried on with their work without complaint and with only occasional sickness absence that might be attributed to their nervous troubles. About 6 per cent suffered from symptoms of a degree that would send others to the consulting-room of the specialist, yet they were at work.

Much depends upon the nature of the work and its environment. An example will illustrate this:

"Laundry worker, female, aged thirty-four, married, four children. Likes the work very much. Would not change it if given the chance. 'My nerves are all bad. The least worry makes me go all of a shake. I worry at the least thing. I'm afraid in the dark or of being alone. Wouldn't go along a dark road.' Describes claustrophobia. 'Should worry and fidget in this room. Never go in a bus; wouldn't go alone in a train; feeling

of being observed; never go out by myself.' She has to find a
companion to accompany her to work. A summons to see her
manager would make her go all hot. Never goes to the pictures.
Is asocia!."

This woman was able to carry on without her employers
suspecting that there was anything wrong with her. Now, as
compared with those in some other occupations, laundry workers
are a cheerful and contented group. Their work is satisfying
inasmuch as each worker sees a material result of her efforts
and knows for herself whether it is well or ill done. The industry
is a flourishing one and no one need stay in a particular laundry
if for any reason she desires a change—and such liberty is
worth a lot, especially to the nervous person. Moreover, there
is a friendly spirit among the workers and an absence of the
social on-guardness that might mark the inhabitants of the
same streets who had chosen an occupation on a presumably
higher grade. This woman is happy in that environment and
so long as her symptoms are tolerated and do not interfere she
is able to enjoy it. If, however, she were a waitress or a typist
she might not be able to meet the demands of even a mild
degree of responsibility towards people and would suffer a
"nervous breakdown."

On the other hand there are symptoms that in themselves
are disabling whatever the occupation. Some of the obsessional
troubles described in the previous section interfere so much
with all activities that external conditions have little influence:
the disability is all-pervading.

One might lay down the rule that in any nervous breakdown
there is an inverse relation between the inner difficulties and the
external stress. This was shown in the war cases, where men
with severe inner difficulties or symptoms might break down
when the sergeant shouted at them on the drill ground, whilst
the stable personalities were able to withstand years of strenuous
experience even if a breakdown occurred in the end. I wrote
in 1919, "the study of a few cases of this type leads me to
believe that, given enough of the strain of modern warfare, any
man whatsoever will eventually break down."

It is unusual for a psychoneurotic patient to describe in

detail his life troubles, and for this reason I reproduce the autobiography of the victim of a war psychoneurosis, although the social conditions concerned belong to a period now past.[1] This man arrived at a home hospital with tremors and an expostulatory stammer that made understanding difficult. After writing out his life history and discussing his troubles he lost his stammer, became cheerful, and developed a sound view of life. His literary style is crude, but direct and sometimes vigorous, and suggests that he had capabilities that with less ill-fortune might have led to success in life. The amount of external stress he suffered is, let us hope, without parallel to-day, but several points in the story will illustrate general principles that are worth mention:

"I begin as a boy going to school and living with my mother under the persecution of great restrictions, very little was a fault. Mind you, she was a clean, hard-working woman, and when she sent us out clean, we must come back the same way. Now I could never do that and I generally got more than I bargained for. Well, that made me worse, for I could never see the sense of it, young as I was, when I could see other boys having such freedom. Many a time I have slept out as I was feared to go home. I see myself even five minutes before my time but I am a long way from home, I won't venture in, another two or three nights sleeping out. I do this rather than take the punishment, and so my life goes on. I am being wakened up to go for milk at 6 o'clock in the morning. It is dark, and I am afraid to go where she wants me. I am supposed to go for a mile into the country where you get most for your money, but the nearest place was mine, and I would make up the shortage with water. It was fear that makes me do this, I was very much afraid. When I was a boy, anyone to make a peculiar face at me, I would run away home crying, of course as I grew up I got away from it. Now I am going to Academy School and I must be home very quick, otherwise the same result, and when I did come home from school very little pleasure was there for me. 'Get the coals out,' the firewood, everything and anything there was found for me to do, boots to be

[1] From the author's *Psychoneuroses of War and Peace.* 1920.

cleaned for all in the house and also the clogs for the work, when doing all this I could hear my school fellows at play outside.

"Now I begin to take and study all this and I come to the conclusion I won't suffer it. I get reckless, I get into the habit I take my own time, and go home when I think fit, but not without suffering for it, and I take another turn or two at sleeping out. This persecution goes on until I am in the sixth standard. I have never absented myself from school in my life, so one morning they have me running messages until I am late for school. I turns back when I get the length of the school, and takes the notion I will run away; I starts, I walks to ——, twenty-three miles away, without a bite to eat, footsore and wearied, I get layed down in an old house under repairs, wakens up early morning faint with hunger. I goes out into the town, I meets a policeman, I tells him my story, and he gives me a penny to buy two rolls. I recollects I have an Auntie staying at ——. I makes my way there, she takes me in and gives me a good breakfast and pays my fare back home, but I am afraid of what the consequences may be, I sleep out again for some nights. Someone must have seen me as I was awakened by my stepfather at 6 o'clock in the morning. Well, you will understand how I felt, he takes me home. I ought to have mentioned that I would be about seven years of age when my stepfather married my mother and I thought he was as strict as her. Well, he took me home, but none of them touches me, and my mother gives me my breakfast. I wonder what's coming next, I can hardly take my breakfast for fear. However, breakfast finished, get yourself washed, that done he takes me to his work where he is foreman in a factory, and starts me on a spinning granny.

"This is alright for a while, then some more what I thought hard knocks; if he caught any of us larking about, it was always me had to suffer for it, and always before my fellow-workers until this became unbearable to me. I takes myself in hands and bears myself out of it on the quiet; I can see myself in my bare feet running to catch the wagonettes going to —— Fair. I gets sat down on the hind step and I am on my way to the Fair. I go eagerly looking for someone to fee me; I am in luck, I gets a fee for £5 and I get 1s. earl money. I feel proud, and yet I am not without that fear, I hang about the town until night until the wagonettes will be going back, I manage home in the same way, but dare not venture home. I go to my grand-mother's and tells her what I have done, and the good old soul looked after me until I should go away to my new place. How I see myself on my journey there, I look back at the old town my heart in my mouth, it goes from my sight, then I cry for a long while. I am nearing my destination, and I begin to wonder what kind of people they are, will they be hard on me. I land at the station. The woman that gave me my fee and 1s. earl money is there to meet me, I get my little tin box on to the trap, then she asks me is that all, I am scarcely able to answer her; on my journey there my thoughts are travelling fast. I feel inclined to jump off and make my way back to where I left. I land at the farm about 11 o'clock, I am showed my sleeping apartment which happens to be above the stables. Then I get my first job, a thing I have never done before and knew absolutely nothing about. I am taken into an old shed where there is an old sow and its litter of pigs. The sow is not able to rise and I am told to keep lifting the little brutes forward to suck her. The old sow would grunt, I would run off like the very devil himself was after me; the mistress sees me, I am trembling from head to foot and she comes and asks me what's wrong with me. I manage to tell her and she bursts out laughing. This I can't stand; here I am I think from bad to worse, and I tell her I am going away in the morning, but she overcomes me by a little gentleness and goes with me back to the pigs, yet I am feared though she is with me. She goes to leave me there again but I leave also so she gives me some other job and looks after the pigs herself, and I may say I am thankful. I am wondering will I be able to stick it, now I have come here. However, I was able to stop nine months altogether and many hardships I suffered during the winter because I was very unprepared against the cold winter blasts.

"Now I left this place in disgust one Monday morning, just through the mistress getting on to me through not having the horse and trap yoked for her at 12 o'clock on the Sunday. Well, I may state that this was her father's fault, who had countermanded the order telling me to wait until they came

C

home from church. There I stood taking all her rage, quaking in my boots, and unable to tell her how it happened I had not done so. I sit down and cry bitterly until I feel ill and sick at heart. On Monday morning I seek what wages are due, they refuse me at first, but in the afternoon she comes and gives me my wages which I think was £7 altogether. This cheered me up so much, this seemed a fortune to me. I gets my little tin box and makes back home and goes straight to my mother's not feared as I knew the £7 was a good introduction for me. Things were alright for me for a week or two, I have always been very forgiving and sometimes I would see these things were my own fault, my mind would again change and tell me they were not my fault, and so my life goes on, the same old restrictions begin at home again, but I don't suffer them long. I makes off again back to farm service for a little over two years without going back home. I had no wish to go back as I never seemed to gain much pleasure there, but yet I was good enough to send a little of my wages to them.

"Now, my ambition craves for something better, so I gets the paper and looks up the vacancy column and gets my eye on the thing that I think I would like, that was young lad wanted to look after two horses and traps for posting, lad from the country preferred. I gets the job alright, but I shall not mention any name here as the boss was a drunken scoundrel and a pure wastrel. I got on with the mistress and I was always sorry for her, she was so good to me, and I stayed there for about a year and six months. I need not go into the torments of this situation as I had many, I stuck it for the poor woman's sake, until I could not suffer this man and his rotten ways no longer. I made the resolution to get out of it as soon as possible. So my chance came when driving a certain gentleman, who told me of a place that was vacant in —— and he asked me would I care to tackle it. Of course I jumped at the opportunity. Well, about a week later I gets a letter from the boss of this place asking for an interview. Of course I have to tell a few lies to my mistress regards this interview, I goes and sees this place, gets the job and promises to be there in three days, but I don't know how I am going to break the news to this poor woman, as she had been so good to me when I had pleurisy she kept me all the time for about eight weeks, and paid the doctor all expenses. All this came up in mind and that man of hers carried on the business but not without coming home drunk every day, and fetching in very little money to her, then I seemed to think that there was to be nothing but trouble, no matter what position I have had, no matter where I went. Now it comes to telling her I am leaving and going to another place. I see tears in her poor eyes, she is crying and I cry also, and on the point of not going; but this woman has better courage than myself, she says to me, 'Go, Will, if you are bettering yourself, I know it has not been much pleasure for you with that man of mine,' and praises me for my work rendered her under what was very trying circumstances.

"Now I am going to my new situation, and it does not turn out too well either. This man does not turn out any better than the one in my last situation, and there is larger responsibilities attached to this place. I am in charge of fourteen horses all very good cattle and there is other two men forby myself. It was the mistress that put me in charge. My boss was about seventeen stone and very tall and all he was good for was eating and drinking, coming in with the horse's knees broken. Sometimes I would have to send another man to fetch him home in his drunken state, perhaps the shafts broken or some other thing, me myself working night and day until I become tired of him and his rotten ways, and makes away from it absolutely fed up.

"I next try the railway, I get a job as porter-signalman on the —— Railway. I am sent to —— station. The first one I come in contact with is the stationmaster, half-drunk, lifting the tickets; more misery for me. Now I have managed to learn to work the signal box, and I get shifted to a signal box at ——; my first night on is on a Friday night, and the box must be washed out, the man I am relieving stays a little while whilst I take off a few trains, then he leaves me. Whenever he goes there is a fear attached to me, yet why it should be so I can't tell, so I starts to wash the floor to help take away this fear; whilst doing this there is a goods train taking on full wagons and leaving empties; I have two trains belled on to me, I take them on, I go on with the floor washing, then I hears three whistles as if for me to close the points, the next thing I hear is a crash and I see the guard running down to the box. He tells me I have fouled both main lines and there I am, with two passenger trains taken on. I run to the phone and tells both boxes to stop both trains, lines are fouled, after that I am useless, fit for nothing, another man is put in the box and the stationmaster takes me to his house and trys to soothe me down. I am court martialled over this and has to appear before all the directors, but I was favoured to have sitting on the Court, District Superintendent —— who came only six miles from my native home. I mind the last question I was asked, have I ever been seriously hurt about the head any time. I told him about my brother letting me fall forty feet and had been carried home as dead. I don't remember any of this incident of my life. However, I was reduced to a carriage cleaner only, for things might have been worse for me; a fortnight I hand in my notice.

"You see I have always been in trouble and you are only getting part, for my mind wanders too quickly for me to give you my life in real rotation, all I can say it has been a very trying life for me. Now I make for Port Glasgow, I see there is a checker wanted in a boat yard. I go and apply for the situation. Mind you, I have never been in a boat yard, but from one or two I knew I gathered many hints regards the principal work of checking, and I was not long in picking the whole thing up. There was about six boats going up at the time, and the job was very worrying to me as I had about twelve men removing all this stuff and you were at everybody's beck and call, one cursing you here, can't get such a thing, and another shouting and cursing for something else, until it got my nerves would not stand it, I never could face trouble like other people, therefore I gave it up, and goes away, very heartless, just feel I could end it all, just as I feel now. However, I make another attempt to get a job as conductor on the cars running between —— and ——. Whilst on this job, I become infatuated with a woman who is now my present wife, then my worst trouble began. I was not a week married until her good brother and sister family came and stayed with me for a week without any invitation at that. When they left she came crying to me, and said something to me in her pitiful way, perhaps I thought I was married to her family. Me the simpleton told her not to bother about it, I was not man enough to put my foot down on it right, therefore I have to suffer the consequences in the near future.

"Next thing that happens is her other sister takes a place in ——, runs away from it, and I get her to keep for a month and you will understand I was not very able to do this on a conductor's wages which was about 22s. weekly. This goes on until I am getting bills from this one and that one which is impossible for me to meet. With that I sell off and run away out of it. I make to my brother's in —— and my wife and I lodge there for a week. I get another start in ——'s steelworks, I don't wish to impose on my brother's goodness so I rents a bare room off another party, there is nothing but a bed in it and the four bare walls to look at. I make another start to gather together a few more things and stores them until I get a house of my own again. Here we are settled down as I fancy once more, but not for long, the bills I have left behind are chasing me up, I am brought to court through the lot, decrees are brought out against me. I have one boy of my own now to keep, but that does not prevent her youngest sister to come and stay with me, until she finds a place. I want to put my foot down here, but instead I simply suffer it, God knows I must be a weak fool. Here I was, bills coming in to me, threatening letters and all sorts of troubles facing me, walking out of one trouble into another.

"I began to lose heart altogether. I get tired of life, I feel I want to get away somewhere by myself, out of it altogether, yet what about my little boys. I must struggle on, yet I must leave my job, arrestments on my wages. I remove again to a country village called ——, a very small place, and I now make a start in a tubework, but I have lost all interest, I am working away here in absolute misery. I cannot make it explicit how I felt. Here my wages were arrested if I made anything over a pound, so I just worked the pound, when I done this here, what belongings I had were taken and sold, I go home from my work, find my house emptied, my three boys sitting all bewildered, and to be asked, 'Father, why have they taken all our things away?' Can you wonder now at my nerves giving way? I attend the doctor here, he gives me tonics for a long while and gives me his advice until I break down completely one morning. I am getting ready to go to work, I have an excruciating pain comes into my head. I see the window flying from me. My next experience is to see my wife bending over me, I go to get up, I find I can't use my right leg and my right arm, she calls on her next door neighbour, and they rub my arm and leg, which brought back the feeling into it. I get up, I am all in a tremble, just the same tremble I took when up the lines, the same fear, I had always headaches, noises in my ears and always in a world of my own. This lasted for over a year and Professor —— was my doctor. My knees went as you see them, but not quite so bad and shaking. When I was getting a bit better he advised me to try and get an outside situation so I got a traveller's place, where I had only four days in the week. I explained to my master my recent trouble and he was a gentleman, with his help and advice I got on every day. After that my wages were good, and I had bonus and commission every quarter, I must say I was never happier in all my life. I was able to throw off the most of my debts, I saw my boys getting justice, the sun seemed to shine.

"All at once I was called to the colours; my spirits go down but I try my best to overcome this feeling, and face it out, but every day that fear again begins to get hold of me, these thoughts of the past get their grip both morally and domestic until I get amongst the shells. I lose my sleep and go off my meat, and then here I am putting my horses in the water tank, a shell bursts with a terrible crash, my horse plunges and gallops away from me. I seem to be rooted to the ground trembling from head to foot, the fragments all landing around me. After that, no matter what sound I heard I am ducking, expecting to be blown to pieces every minute, and I begin to get so confused and stupid it ends with major and quartermaster taking me up before the doctor. The next I am sent off to the clearing station. Now I have given you my story to the best of my ability with many instances missed out. Had I tried to keep up with my mind I should have mixed it all up together. Mind, I have not given any of my evil parts as that is and must be between me and my Maker. How I have managed to write as much as I have done is what I believe is your will and not mine, and to be candid with you I should like to go back to that short life of pleasure as a traveller again which was ended all so quick, just where I was beginning to see life in a more happier sphere and getting away from all my troubles. Believe me, I should not like to have any more of it."

The first thing of note is that one can understand this case with little appeal to psychoanalytical principles. Pitiful as the story is, typical psychoneurotic symptoms appear only on three occasions; when he developed a hysterical paralysis of the right side and was always in a world of his own (perhaps this was a spell of de-personalization); when he experienced a phobia immediately before the railway accident; and when his tremors and stammer appeared. The phobia is accurately described when he writes, ". . . there is a fear attached to me, yet why it should be so I can't tell." It should be contrasted with his fear after the shell-burst, the cause of which was quite clear to him. Notable items are the prescription of tonics by the doctor, and the question about injury to his head at the time of the railway accident, both of them characteristic of a time when medical psychology was known only to a few. The same can be said about his enlistment into a fighting force, for one aim of psychiatry in the last war was to anticipate and prevent the exposure of such men to conditions that would inevitably result in their becoming a burden to the Army.

His power of recuperation shows itself more than once and, though the conclusion might not be obvious at first sight, I judge that this man started life with a fairly healthy mental and emotional equipment and broke down because of external stress operating from his early days. He presents an example of a case that could be successfully handled without resort to psychoanalytical procedure.

The maternal strictness and absence of affection set a reaction pattern that persisted throughout life. His response to any overbearing treatment was to endure it or run away; when his first mistress, who had treated him gently in the matter of the pigs, scolds him without reason he is too scared to stand up for himself and decides to leave. So he acts in all his difficulties, and his story becomes monotonous in that respect. This persistence of an infantile reaction throughout life is a commonplace, though it must be pointed out that there is here no evidence of infantile amnesia as playing any part in the maintenance of the symptoms. There is a surprising absence of psychoneurotic symptoms except on the three occasions noted above. Except for those three occasions his reactions were fully accounted for by rational and conscious motives, so there is little need for psychoanalytical explanations.

The next account is a contrast, in which, though the information is limited to what could be discovered in a single interview, we can read a story of nervous symptoms interfering with all the activities of an ordinary life, there being no indication of external stress except a dislike of her occupation.

"Female clerk, aged thirty-three. Dislikes the work. A month ago was away for 'nerves.' Had made a mistake and it worried her. Always had feared the dark or being alone. Nervous if spoken to by strangers. Cinemas try her eyes. Has good and bad days. No energy; improves as the day goes on; has a feeling of 'something awful going to happen—a cloud.' Tennis is too much for her; influenza left her heart weak. (Asked how that showed itself.) Goes faint in trains and crowds. Could not sit in a small room like this; it would make her come over all faint; no, not frightened at all; it's the heart. Wears weak glasses to avoid strain and headache. Had all her teeth out for gastritis before age of twenty-one. Hands are blue. Does not look forward to staying on for her pension. Talks frankly about shortage of men, but declares indifference."

Here we see the conversion of phobias into physical symptoms; the cinema touches up various phobias in nervous people, but this patient keeps away from it because it affects her eyes—this enables her to avoid confession of fears, or perhaps to hide them from herself by a process of dissociation. Similarly a typical claustrophobia, a train phobia and a phobia of crowds, are camouflaged as a weak heart. The gastritis corresponds to a "psychosomatic disorder" in which the emotional disturbance produces a digestive symptom the true origin of which is unrecognized, and the blue hands indicate a similar interference with the circulation. The month's absence was a mild breakdown, the psychological nature of which was admitted.

What was behind all this can only be surmised. There may have been home difficulties serving as constant irritants, but our Scottish friend would have dealt with them rather than be driven into such a mess of nervous symptoms. I picture a narrow upbringing with emotional taboos and inhibitions that made the world something to be dreaded rather than enjoyed, but the deeper unconscious roots of her trouble could be revealed only by analysis. The only external factor to be recognized is the realization of the tedium of a life of clerical routine that will last till pensionable age is reached, but although that may now be operative it would not account for the gastritis twelve years earlier.

The influence of tedium combined with the prospect of a pension produced what seemed at first sight to be a paradoxical result in an industrial enquiry I once helped to carry out. A group of entrants in an occupation that provided these two factors was investigated psychologically and its members sorted out according to the presence or absence of fairly severe nervous symptoms, and after ten years reports were made as to their progress. To the surprise of some people, all but one of those with symptoms were still at the job and received favourable reports from their superiors, whilst, of the supposedly healthy, a large proportion had left the work and few received full marks for efficiency. This was, however, not a surprise to the investigators, who already knew that the middle-aged workers in that occupation contained an excess of nervous subjects as compared with the general working population; but they had been puzzled as to how or when the selection of nervous workers took place, since it is not in accord with theory that the nature of the employment should be expected to produce symptoms in the emotionally stable. The solution of the puzzle was now plain. Some of the active and enterprising young people of either sex, free of hampering symptoms or inhibitions, had decided that the safe and tedious life was not for them. Others had taken the easier course of sticking to the job, and reacted to its tedium by a more or less healthy discontent. But the nervous worriers, the boys tied to the mother's apron-strings, the girls who dreaded a world full of unknown and unspecified possibilities, thought to find a safe haven in the routine task and assured security. Yet, as the last case cited above shows, the time comes when security palls and a sense of frustration creeps in. When that happens we may expect nervous troubles, from manifestations of apparent physical disease to straightforward nervous breakdown.

c*

CHAPTER IV

DISSOCIATION

DISSOCIATION

THERE is a group of mental phenomena that can be conveniently studied as taking place in accordance with a theory first propounded by Pierre Janet of Paris. That is the theory of *dissociation of consciousness*.

When we wake in the morning we begin to think, and, unless we fall asleep or otherwise become unconscious, there is a constant stream of mental activity all day long. Into this stream come impressions from outside and memories from within; apparently aimless day-dreaming or intensely concentrated thinking may go on in it, and we are aware of it at any moment. That is the stream of consciousness, and we tend to think that it represents all our mental processes. But in all of us there are easily to be recognized mental activities of which we are not fully aware. As you read this book you shift in your chair. Did you know you were moving? Or why you moved? Or perhaps you find yourself humming a tune, and only by taking thought can you recognize that some chance association with words you have read called up the tune and started you humming it. It is plain that besides the main stream of consciousness there are subsidiary trickles about which you know very little. Habitual actions, like dressing or undressing, are carried out with the minimum of awareness, as if one action automatically called up the next: (if I change my clothes in the daytime I always start winding up my watch as if I am going to bed). A good example of such action, so automatic that we are quite unaware of it, is shown when, as we cross a road and approach the kerb, we shorten or lengthen our stride so that we place the oncoming foot squarely on the kerb, never placing it awkwardly on the edge. We can watch a toddler giving full attention to the placing of his foot, but in us grown-ups the perception of distance and the adjustment of our stride is carried on with little or no awareness.

A routine task involving fairly elaborate thinking can be carried out whilst another stream of thought is active. I have been assured by competent shorthand-typists that they can type from their notes and at the same time busy themselves with more interesting themes, such as plans for the next week-end or the possibilty of a new hat. In this case we may ask which is the main stream and which is the subsidiary, and I regard the planning stream as the main one, the other more nearly approaching the automatic.[1] This is confirmed by the fact that some typists declare that if all goes smoothly they can type from their notes without paying conscious attention to the sense of the words unless some difficulty arises, when all their attention becomes directed to it.

From this it is but a step to automatic writing, in which the performer pursues some conscious activity, such as reading, whilst allowing his hand, provided with a pencil, to rest upon a paper, the hand and paper sometimes being screened from his observation. If the experiment succeeds the hand writes without the operator consciously directing it, and coherent script may be produced. Though I have never seen automatic writing done, yet ample and reliable evidence has been given that leaves no doubt as to its occurrence. Some psycho-therapists have made use of automatic writing as a means of mental exploration, but the nearest I have seen to it was a chance action of an ex-service patient who had been a prisoner-of-war, and, among other symptoms, had complained of troubles in his marital relations that almost amounted to complete impotence.

He was talking about prison camp experiences and of the behaviour of the German guards, and casually told how different units were distinguished by what he called tassels on their bayonets. At this he produced a pencil and, using a card that chanced to lie on the table, made a sketch of the bayonet and tassels. Still talking he went on "doodling," appar-

---

[1] I obtained this information in the course of investigations in industrial psychology. The fact emerged that this "division of attention," as it may be called, was characteristic of the competent worker. The girl who said, "Oh, no! I always concentrate on my work," was making heavy weather of the job and often turned out to be suffering from nervous symptoms which tended to interfere with efficiency.

ently haphazardly, till I pulled him up and said, "Now, look at that card. What have you drawn?" He looked, and gasped in horror, for he had covered it with sketches of the crudest and rudest schoolboy obscenities, which proved of great value in loosening up early recollections that helped him considerably.

In automatic writing we approach the abnormal, and can picture it as dependent upon two simultaneous streams of consciousness having no joint awareness; indeed, a temporary dissociation of personality.

HYSTERIA AS A DISSOCIATION

Pierre Janet, (who, by the way, formulated this theory fifty years ago and is still alive and active)[1] applied this idea of dissociation to help in the understanding of hysteria and related conditions.

There have been innumerable attempts to define hysteria. The word first conveyed the idea of the unsatisfied and wandering womb as the cause of trouble, and not so long ago we were told that Adolf Hitler used to chew the carpet in a fit of hysteria. Besides these two rather remotely connected behaviour patterns are all sorts of apparently unrelated phenomena such as fits of wandering or inability to speak above a whisper. In spite of all this tangle the reader probably has his own ideas about hysteria and is prepared to make use of the word as if he knows what he means by it. Hence it is very dangerous indeed for a doctor to make the diagnosis and I should like to abolish the word, with its mixture of superstition, up-to-date ignorance, and moral condemnation. There is still freely expressed the view that hysteria is merely unconscious malingering and I will plead guilty to having held that view myself at one time, and, even when satisfied that it was false, I still had difficulty in approaching the hysteric with that equanimity so necessary to understanding. A grasp of Janet's theory of dissociation exorcised from me the last of that moral judgement.[2]

[1] His death at the age of eighty-seven occurred since this was written.
[2] Here I may owe some apology to my psychiatric friends who still make play with the conditioned reflex. They may be unwittingly setting up a guard

I shall not be unorthodox if I define hysteria as a symptom or group of symptoms that can be regarded as a dissociation of consciousness, the dissociated stream bearing within it elements of which the main stream is unaware.

This is apparently a departure from Freud's belief in the unconscious as the source of the psychoneurotic symptom, but it is not in any way a contradiction of it. Dissociation gives a fancied picture of *what* is happening on a fairly superficial level of the mind; it gives no picture showing *why* it happens: if we want an answer to that question we must turn to psychoanalytical conceptions for it. The dyed-in-the-wool psychoanalyst, however, finds little or no use for the dissociation theory. He declares that in some published cases of hysterical double personality its development has been unwittingly encouraged by the observer, and that in the hands of the psychoanalyst this development would not have taken place. I agree with this, for, although I do not accept the facile explanation of "suggestion" or "auto-suggestion" as the cause of hysteria, yet on reading some accounts of double personality I have had to recognize that the observer and patient worked together in building it up. This process of building up occurs in the development of some mediums, but, as will be seen in the examples given below, the hysterical dissociation is in being when the patient first comes under observation. The forgetting of an unpleasant memory may be regarded either as a repression into the unconscious or as a dissociation of consciousness: if the memory is of something that should ordinarily be accessible—the memory of an episode a few months or years ago, for example—then it is convenient to picture the condition as a dissociation: if it is of a childhood episode, then it is more convenient to picture the memory as lying in the unconscious.

The unconscious contains, besides the memory of events, the memory of desires, frustrations, emotions and phantasies,

against the moral judgement that might be aroused if they regarded the psychoneurosis as something the man-as-a-whole is producing. After all, dissociation is a picture of mechanism like the conditioned reflex. The difference is that I know my picture is only a useful conception and not a statement of material happenings; the conditioned reflex is declared to be a material happening, even when made to account for all human behaviour.

and also active urges towards behaviour of a particular kind. The dissociated stream likewise has a far greater content than merely the memory of events; indeed, it has all the qualities and capacities of the main stream except that of awareness. Some actual cases will illustrate these points, and war provides such clear-cut examples that I make no apology for turning to that source. This last war has already produced the same sort of case material.

"A man with a record of over a year of strenuous fighting had an obvious hysterical paralysis of the arm when admitted to a home hospital. Asked about his war experiences, he at once declared that he never thought about them, they never worried him, he was never afraid, and if it were not for his paralysed arm he would be back with his mates in France. Instead of being argued with about this last statement, he was told that the paralysis was not due to any physical cause but was probably associated with something that had happened in France. He was intelligent and co-operative and agreed to tell of his war doings. Straightway he found, to his own surprise, that he could remember very little about them. He was then started at a point where his loss of memory began and, with eyes closed, made to talk of his doings in the present tense, as if they were happening again. This simple technique, which is forgotten now that drugs are used for such revival, carried him past the barrier and he went on to recapitulate, with appropriate emotion, the terrifying incidents of warfare that he had dissociated (or repressed). Several sittings were needed to cover the whole ground: on each occasion he was made to sit up after the recapitulation and, with open eyes and therefore in full contact with the present, discuss the episodes and the emotions he experienced. The explanation of the paralysis came when he told of his particular chum being wounded in the arm and sent down the line; he had in a way identified himself with his chum and given himself a corresponding disability. With this realization the paralysis disappeared.

"Meanwhile he had shown himself a willing worker, grateful for his treatment. One day I asked him, 'What about going back to France?' to receive at once the answer, 'If I

went back up the line I should run like a rabbit.' Then I
showed him my entry in his case-notes: 'Says he was never
afraid,' and he answered, 'Well, sir, when I said that I believed
it.'"

This man was neither a fool nor a rogue, and his last
statement is a striking expression of how he recognized the
nature of his past dissociation and the fact that his personality
was now integrated. He was, however, still afraid. If it is said
that, because of that fear, he was not cured, the answer would
be that a deep analysis might have revealed why fear came upon
him to such a degree, and perhaps what was the unconscious
nature of his attachment to his chum; such analysis might
have made him fit for fighting again or it might not, but it was
for practical reasons out of the question, and we had to be
satisfied that his hysterical paralysis was removed and not
likely to be replaced by another symptom.

We can specify some of the contents of his dissociated
stream. They were:

(i) The war memories.
(ii) His fear.
(iii) The knowledge that the paralysis served to remove
him from the front line.
(iv) The muscular control that maintained the paralysis.

If all the elements of this stream had been present in full
awareness then he would have been a malingerer. Why were
they not thus present? He was at heart a good soldier and a
decent citizen; there was conflict between that side of him and
the growing inability any longer to carry on as a front line
soldier. That conflict was solved by the dissociation and the
paralysis.

His denial of fear was diagnostic of a dissociation. His
conflict was solved, his fear split off or repressed, and so long as
the paralysis could be maintained, "everything in the garden
was lovely." It can be understood that if the paralysis had been
removed by any other method than the re-association of the
dissociated fears and memories, some other symptoms would
have arisen. This sequence was a commonplace, and with

experience one came to recognize that the removal of a hysterical symptom might be the beginning of treatment rather than the end. The next case, which I met with in my surgical days, taught me that lesson in a way I shall never forget:

"A colonel came to my hospital for massage and electrical treatment after a wound of the arm. After a course of this treatment, rather perfunctorily supervised, I recognized a hysterical paralysis and with some trepidation the temporary captain essayed to treat the hysteria of the colonel. I explained, as an honest surgeon would, that he had a fixed idea he could not move the arm, there was no real cause for the paralysis, and he had better go away and try a game of billiards. He said he would gladly follow my advice, for the Army was his livelihood and he feared being invalided out of the service by a medical board before which he was to appear within a fortnight. The game of billiards worked, he was passed fit for foreign service, and wrote me a grateful letter from France.

"Later on, when I was in France myself, I read in the paper that he had been invalided home, bedridden from paralysis. He had been visited by a specialist (with whom I afterwards discussed the case), and after his departure this bedridden cripple got up, went into the next room, found his revolver, and shot himself. My satisfaction had been premature, and a retrospect of the case recalls many traits in the patient—over-scrupulousness, hesitancy of speech, peculiar little tics—which marked him as a sufferer from pathological doubts and fears, against which he was carrying on a single-handed fight and which finally defeated him. When the specialist made clear to him that he had again produced a spurious paralysis he was so overwhelmed with shame that he killed himself."

This kind of hysterical symptom was very common in the first World War, and comparatively uncommon in this last. There is little doubt that nowadays both these patients would have been recognized as in need of psychiatric investigation before the onset of the hysterical symptom. Certainly no modern psychiatrist would have treated the unfortunate colonel as I did.

The diminished number of hysterical symptoms in the last war is due to two causes: the elimination from the front line troops of a fair number of nervous people who would have quickly broken down, and the recognition of impending or actual breakdown in those who had reached their limit and needed rest, treatment, or perhaps removal to the base. A hysterical symptom is likely to arise if these needs are not recognized.

The next case shows another kind of symptom that dissociated memories can produce:

"The patient arrived direct from France in a confused state. He would answer questions if addressed sharply and was able to say where he was but talked continually of falling aeroplanes, calling out the names of the actual victims. I ordered him to be dressed, and other patients took him to the recreation hut where, becoming interested in the music of a gramophone, he returned to a full knowledge of his surroundings. Next day he easily recalled the incidents of which he had spoken whilst in the confused state.

"Two days later came a moonlight night, the first since his return to England. At moonrise he was noticed to be in a somnambulism; he was very agitated and went out of doors. Here he scanned the sky, saying: 'He's not back. That's a German; the searchlight's got him; he's dropped six.' This condition lasted for two hours, during which he was put to bed and watched for more information. At last he said, with great relief, 'Here he is,' and immediately lay back and went into a natural sleep. Next day he easily recalled, from the above phrases, a forgotten incident when a pilot went up for a quarter-hour practice flight by moonlight and, losing the aerodrome, was up for two hours. The aerodrome showed signals, bringing along a German plane which dropped six bombs. The somnambulism lasted about the same time as the incident reproduced, and reproduction was exact, there being no distortion."

The memories formed the main stream when he was admitted; they claimed his awareness, which could only with difficulty be brought to the actual present. When his awareness was at last fixed on reality the dissociated memories were dormant for a time, but with the moonlight as a stimulus they took complete control and it was impossible to bring his attention back to his real surroundings. Yet he must have perceived those surroundings, for he could walk about, avoid obstacles, and even be persuaded to go back to bed. Bringing the recollection into full consciousness the next day was essential to prevent repetition of the somnambulism; once properly integrated with his personality it was harmless.

This last episode was a somnambulism, a condition of dissociation in which the patient is plainly not behaving with full awareness of his surroundings. But it is possible for a person to be so in contact with his surroundings, although living in a state of dissociation, that his condition would not be noticed by a chance observer. This is called a fugue. He is generally under the influence of some desire or fantasy that has been excluded from ordinary consciousness and now invades it, to take complete direction of his activities. There is often some internal conflict, or even an offence approaching criminality, from which the fugue may be an apparent means of escape, for it generally involves a wandering away. An example often cited is the case, described by William James, of Ansel Bourne, an American clergyman who wandered off and "came to" after some months, to find himself in charge of a small shop but with no recollection of how he came to be there. In those days nothing was known about methods of restoring the memory of the fugue, but they are now commonplace, and the following case of my own is not so remarkable as it might appear:

"R.T., a clerk, aged twenty-seven, living in London, had lost several situations by suddenly absenting himself from work for periods of a few days up to a fortnight. On each occasion he found himself, footsore and travel-stained, somewhere in the Midlands with no recollection of how he reached there, his 'coming to' being accompanied by a feeling as of a crash inside his head. Sometimes he walked home or sought a lift from lorry drivers, but finally he learnt to seek the aid of the local police, and I was able to get into touch with one police surgeon who gave me a description of the patient's condition on an occasion when he found himself in Oxfordshire. The first recognized fugue occurred during actual warfare, when the man, who was on telephone duty close to the front-line trenches, found himself several miles behind the lines. He 'pulled himself together' and returned to duty without his absence being discovered. After being invalided to England for gastritis (almost certainly a neurosis), he was sent to a training camp on the South coast and puzzled the military authorities by next appearing in the neighbourhood of Calais with no explanation of how he crossed the Channel. His account of himself was finally accepted, and he was returned to England.

"When he came under treatment he described a recent fugue that had begun in the neighbourhood of King's Cross Station, the amnesia extending from the purchase of a newspaper—the last recollection before the fugue—to the recovery of ordinary consciousness early one morning in a field near Bedford. It was decided to attack this loss of memory, so he was placed on a couch and directed to imagine and describe himself going through his actions just before the purchase of the paper. With suitable stimulation he carried on the recapitulation to the purchase of a ticket to some place a few miles from London and then went through the whole episode of the fugue, describing minutely how and when he obtained food, where he slept, how he talked to people, and indicating that the fugue was brought to an end by the emptiness of pocket and stomach. The aim of the journey was to reach Wolverhampton, where there lived, he thought, a man who had once befriended him and might perhaps help him again. He was at this time out of work and there seemed no reason why the motive should not have been consciously put into action—except that, judged in the light of common sense, the chance of finding help in Wolverhampton was too remote to justify the journey.

"When the process of recovery had become easier it was possible to recapitulate his trip to Calais. He had imposed upon a sergeant with a tale of lost papers and leave overstayed, and the sergeant had smuggled him across to France among a batch of his own men.

"But the immediate cause of the fugues only came to light with discussion of his domestic life. He had not been on good terms with his wife's family, who had been obliged to contribute to his support and regarded him with hostility. The wife herself made his home life decidedly uncomfortable, and it was when her reproaches became too pungent that the fugues took place. They were, like the original one, a running away from the unbearable, and the fugue to Calais had a similar explanation, though the stimulus was military and not marital.

"With the working out of these memories and the recognition of the causes the fugues ceased, though the man's lack of stamina still remained and he had made but little progress towards rehabilitating himself as a useful citizen when I lost sight of him."

We often read in the papers about people who are taken into hospital suffering from "loss of memory." When these cases are genuine they are usually fugues, but it is probable that they are not often psychologically investigated. The investigation, if successful, establishes their genuineness by reviving the memory. In the following example the episode of recognizing the pocket-knife was a striking example of the completeness of the dissociation in a minute detail:

"A lad of fifteen started off to return to a boarding school by train after the vacation, and was found late at night in a provincial town several miles from the school. When questioned by the police he said that he had landed in England that morning and was thirteen years old. He knew his name and who his parents were, and was put in hospital for the night. A few days later I saw him. He had actually landed here two years before and now he remembered nothing between that time and being found by the police. He told how he had noticed a calendar in the police station and asked if it was correct. It was. 'Then,' said he, 'I must be fifteen.' The police turned out his pockets' and he could identify none of their contents except a pocket-knife. He could not explain this till I asked how long he had had it. Then he realized that he had owned it when he was still abroad. In hospital next morning the visiting physician accused him of having been up to some mischief and advised him to make a clean breast of it. According to the boy's story his answer was materially irrelevant but appropriately rude.

"By use of the method described in the last case he was taken back to breakfast on the ship as it came up the Thames. From that he described landing, passing through the Customs, with remarkable details of every little incident, and finally the taking of a railway journey that ended in the house of a relative. Gradually he filled in the whole of the amnesia and at last could tell conversationally how his life abroad had been full of everything a boy could wish for, but in England he had been profoundly miserable, at cross purposes with a strict parent who appeared to him arbitrary and unreasonable, and equally at cross purposes with his school authorities. On his return to school he had separated himself from his companions, sat alone in a railway carriage feeling sick and miserable, slipped away unnoticed at the school station and then wandered distraught till found by the police. His two years' memories were so distasteful that he had blotted them out completely."

The claim of loss of memory is often regarded as a conscious attempt to escape the responsibility of some misdeed during the amnesic period. That may be true in some cases, and the behaviour of the subject when revival is attempted might throw light upon his genuineness. Full co-operation resulting in a revival that follows a familiar course should be decisive. An offence committed during an undoubted dissociation, with the main personality shut off, might raise some difficult legal questions.

In many of these cases there can be imagined, among the contents of the dissociated stream, something in the nature of a material motive. In the last case there might have been a desire to escape from the unpleasantness of school, though the elaborateness of the loss of memory seems unnecessary if we measure the boy's behaviour by rational standards.

In the next case of amnesia the desire to blot out a distressing memory seems the only imaginable motive and, once the dissociation was established, the results were so unpleasant that the patient could derive only pain from them.

The colleague to whom I am indebted for these notes points out how the nature of the case was not recognized by him in the beginning and that the intelligent co-operation of the patient played a great part in its elucidation.

"A woman, aged thirty-three, had for some months been in a distraught state, unable to stay alone, and complained of what might technically be described as a 'loss of function of the real,' for she declared that nothing seemed real and she went about her duties in an automatic way as if in a dream, This is a distressing state which patients find it very difficult to describe, but is comparatively common.

"She had two boys, aged eleven and six, having lost a girl between these two at the age of eight months from a sudden severe illness. The trouble had come on when her husband was demobilized a few months before, and at first one thought of the possibility of some marital difficulty. Both patient and her husband, however, seemed a straightforward devoted couple. In search for any earlier indications of nervous trouble the patient volunteered that she had not 'been the same' since the birth of her last child, and it soon emerged that she had a loss of memory for everything connected with that birth. Her last memory was of being terribly frightened by the first siren after declaration of war in 1939, of dashing into a neighbour's house, and there sitting by the window for a period that seemed endless whilst everything seemed strange and her mind was full of fear that she would lose her baby. Her baby was born within a few days but she remembered no events till about a month later. She admitted that in her country village she had not thought to be so soon involved in war's alarm, but there was nothing that would account for an apparently happy and well-adjusted woman being so deeply affected, and the loss of memory seemed unaccountable. The attempt to revive it failed, but a chance reference took the search back to the tragically sudden death of the eight-months-old infant two years earlier. Here again was a loss of memory, but it was soon recovered and the patient went through the episode with the liberation of intense emotion and the recapitulation of feelings that it was all unreal, that she would wake up and find everything as before, at the same time knowing that she was deceiving herself and yet unable to break the train of thought or talk about it to anyone. Finally she banished it all from consciousness and took up her ordinary life again.

"Returning to the episode of the siren she now was able to fill in the amnesia, recognizing that she had again been seized by the feeling of unreality coupled with the belief that she would lose her new baby as she had lost the other. The cloud again apparently lifted when this was blotted from her memory.

"She was now able to explain spontaneously what had produced the trouble that had brought her for treatment. With her husband's return had come the possibility of and desire for another child, but that conscious desire had stirred up the dissociated (or, we might say, the repressed) train of memories; all the emotion concerned therewith had risen into consciousness to produce her symptoms. Those she could now recognize as being identical with the old experience, though it may be hard for the reader to grasp that she had been entirely unable, without aid, to trace any connexion with the past and that the symptoms had appeared to her as something new and inexplicable coming entirely out of the blue."

It is rare to meet such a clear-cut case as this, where a perfectly adjusted woman with well-developed affection for husband and family suffers a breakdown through the splitting-off of the memory of one emotional incident. The psychoanalyst might speculate as to an unconscious identification of herself with her girl child, or some other deep-seated primary cause of her excessive reaction to the loss, but there was apparently no need to investigate that possibility.

These examples justify the theory of dissociation as a convenient formula that helps us to understand varieties of abnormal behaviour that might otherwise seem incomprehensible.

Suggestibility in Hysteria

There is another factor in hysteria, the importance of which is estimated very differently by different people; that is, suggestibility. To psychoanalysts it appears as an incidental symptom of little interest, though they believe that some classical cases of hysterical double personality were artificially built up by the physician. On the other hand Babinski, a French neurologist, believed that hysteria was nothing but suggestibility, that all its symptoms were produced by suggestion and could be removed by the same process. It is obvious that, with my belief in psychoanalytical findings, I must reject Babinski's theory.

The subject will be dealt with more fully in the chapter on hypnotism, but meanwhile I must agree that in many hysterical subjects there is a readiness to accept suggestions as to physical symptoms or abnormal behaviour. This readiness would obviously be inoperative if no suggestions were offered, and the psychoanalysts declare that they do not offer such suggestions and therefore they do not see the manifestations to which other clinicians attach so much importance. I agree with this, but as will be seen in the later chapter, the history of the subject is full of instances in which suggestions have been offered and fantastic syndromes (i.e., groups of symptoms) have been built up and accepted in ignorance of their true origin. Charcot's *grande hysterie* and the phenomenon of hysterical anaesthesia—to be described later—are examples of these artificial products.

There has been a recent instance of this building up which may be within the recollection of some of my readers and affords a striking example of the general acceptance of a fictitious symptom produced by suggestion.

In the middle of the last war there appeared in our newspapers pictorial advertisements showing what the nocturnal streets looked like to the night-blind, and what they looked like to people made healthy by something or other out of a bottle. These advertisements suddenly ceased, and behind their appearance and disappearance is a long story.

Night-blindness has occurred as an epidemic in armies since the time of the crusades, and in the 1914–1918 war it was so prevalent in the Continental armies that over forty-five communications about it appeared in French, Belgian, and German medical journals. In our literature it received only one casual mention, for we had apparently escaped the epidemic, the nature of which was very dubious.

There are several physical disorders of the eyes in which night-blindness occurs, and there is good evidence that vitamin defect of severe degree can produce it. Investigations had been carried out to determine whether mild degrees of night-blindness could serve as a measure of vitamin defect, and at the start of the war a good deal of attention was being directed towards the subject. The public were becoming interested, and a medical man wrote in one of our journals drawing attention to the Continental epidemic in the first war and, believing that epidemic to have been fictitious, warned his readers that if we were not careful in our talk about vitamins and night-blindness we might produce an epidemic here. That is precisely what happened, in spite of the warning, and night-blindness became very popular. The advertisements described above now appeared, radio comedians made gags about it, and vitamin fans ate carrots till their skins turned yellow. Soldiers and munition workers went night-blind in large numbers, and learned-looking papers appeared in our medical journals about this result of vitamin defect. At last some psychologically-minded physicians took up the matter, examined sixty-odd soldiers who had the complaint and found nearly all of them to be suffering from psychoneurotic symptoms, hitherto unrecognized, so severe as to render them unfit for service. The night-blindness was only an excrescence upon this psychoneurotic condition and would not have arisen if the opportunity to develop it had not been offered to the patients. Recognition of these facts led to an official but confidential pronouncement that for practical purposes night-blindness did not exist in the absence of gross ocular disease. I rather suspect that the Ministry of Food took a hand at this stage, for a belief in widespread night-blindness due to a dietary defect was a serious matter for them. Whether that was so or not, the advertisements disappeared and both the public and my profession forgot all about war-time night-blindness.[1]

[1] The Continental epidemic of the 1914-1918 war was obviously of the same nature, for, in spite of the expenditure of literary energy, no physical cause was ever discovered. The nature of the other war-time epidemics must remain doubtful, for it is true that vitamin defects bad enough to

Here we see an example of a two-way or reciprocal suggestibility—on the one hand the psychoneurotic patients ready to accept the suggestion of a physical disorder; on the other hand a profession, not yet fully educated in matters psychological, ready to accept in turn the suggestion that a physical disease is present. Yet suggestion had not produced the psychoneurotic disorders from which these soldiers originally suffered; it only supplied a new symptom.

Why was the suggestion accepted? Many of these men were suffering from disabling symptoms that even now are not readily recognized by all medical men. When given the opportunity of honourable escape from the environment that is made difficult or intolerable by their existing symptoms they would seize upon it, and on this occasion night-blindness offered the way out. The situation was the same as that confronting some of the men whose cases were described in the previous chapter in the discussion on compensation neurosis. It is impossible to guess how many of the men really believed in their night-blindness and how many of them knew it was only a roundabout way of expressing their main disability. One possibility, however, was not examined by the investigators, and that is the influence of fear of the dark—a very common symptom of which the victim is generally ashamed. If he is now offered night-blindness as a cover for the fear he would readily accept it, perhaps suppressing his knowledge of the fear, or making it part of a dissociated stream, like the soldier who suppresses his war fears. Always, too, in such episodes as this, there is the possibility of straightforward malingering.

It is noteworthy that there was at first some medical opposition to the psychological view of the nature of the night-blindness; no public pronouncement, however, was made, the cessation of advertisements and of further diagnoses of night-blindness being all that was necessary for public interest in it to come to an end. It is possible that a public declaration as to the nature of the supposed disorder might have stirred up interfere seriously with general health can also produce definite eye troubles, among which night-blindness finds a place. It is reasonable to suppose that some of them at least were of a hysterical nature. The psychoneuroses of war are probably as old as war itself.

indignant resistance, for everyone having a friend or relative afflicted with it would have felt called upon to defend him from a wicked slur upon his personal character. Students of propaganda methods might profit by noting this useful result of negative action.

Serious as this epidemic was, coming as it did in the middle of our war effort, it bears out the psychoanalytical view that suggestibility in hysteria is a secondary manifestation and would remain ineffective as long as the suggestion of further symptoms is avoided.

THOUGHT-READING

Everyone has heard about telepathy, or thought-transference at a distance without the intervention of any sensory perception, and our B.B.C. Brains Trust has more than once discussed it. My mechanistic training still influences me, and I cannot conceive a "thought" as anything that can be thus transferred. Analogies with radio communication and such-like are valid only so far as they justify the "more things in heaven and earth" argument, which can be used to support anything you like. I have read a good deal of the literature on the subject, but the evidence is not strong enough to overcome my prejudice. Still, some of my psychological colleagues believe there is enough evidence to justify further enquiry and I must let it go at that.

Thought-reading, however, is an everyday phenomenon if we consider it as a deduction made from a sensory impression received from another person. The infant in the cradle who returns smile for smile is learning to read thoughts, and adults show a wonderful range of sensitivity towards facial expression as an indication of the thoughts of others. With this is often coupled that faculty sometimes called intuition—a word wrongly conveying, in my opinion, the idea of something independent of reason. Independent of conscious reasoning, yes, but we are agreed that consciousness is only a part of our mind, and just below the level of consciousness processes go on unbeknown to us, only their conclusions making themselves known. Some of us may be able to detect that process when we are faced with a mechanical problem; we stare at it for a time whilst a tangle of thought goes on, and suddenly we see the solution.

Some people have the power of tracking their thoughts backwards from the solution and picking up the threads of the tangle. Here is an example of this tracking back of an "intuition."

A colleague of mine has a sometimes surprising power of jumping to conclusions and then tracing back his own thought processes. One day whilst relating an incident to him I suddenly forgot the name of a participant when it was on the tip of my tongue, and before I could recall the name my colleague supplied it.[1] I had not told him the story before and when I asked how he knew the name of the man he answered "It just came to me." Knowing his peculiarity, I said, "Think it out." After a pause he said, "You don't like him," and I had to admit that I had about this man a peculiar feeling of aversion. "That's it," said he, "you were talking about him some weeks ago and it was the look on your face just now that told me who it was."

Here we have a good example of what might have passed as a case of thought-transference. Call it thought-reading and there is no objection.

Here is a personal example of "intuition."

"In the winter of 1914–1915 I had been in charge of the cerebro-spinal fever wards in a military hospital. The epidemic subsided, as typically happens, when spring came, and I had seen no cases for several months when I chanced to be walking through a medical ward whilst I talked with a colleague. As we were about to leave the ward I was arrested by the thought

---

[1] Freud studied this phenomenon of momentarily forgetting names of people. Using the method of free association he found that it was due to the interference of an unpleasing emotion directly or indirectly stirred by the name, and I am satisfied that this explanation is often true. I do not think it would be true of that forgetting which so often occurs in people of advancing years—unless, perhaps, old people have accumulated so many possibilities of unpleasing emotion that almost any name will call up one of them. Perhaps the reader will share my dislike to accepting that supposition. My sympathies go out to the professor of zoology who protested: "Whenever I remember the name of a student I forget the name of a fish."

that there was a case of cerebro-spinal fever in a bed behind me. I turned back and found that was so, the patient having been admitted with the diagnosis of influenza.

"What had happened in my mind? I had become used to the aspect of a man with this illness; the brow furrowed by headache, the neck rigid and head extended, the immobility of the man whilst he followed me with his eyes. I may never have put into words these and other little points, but I had seen them often enough, and on this occasion if I had stopped by the man's bedside and recognized the disease there would have been no cause for surprise. But I was busy talking; I had paid no conscious attention to the appearance of the man, but somewhere below the level of consciousness— call it in the sub-conscious, the unconscious, or, if you like, picture it as in a dissociated stream of consciousness—there was not only a perception of these signs but a putting of them together and the coming to a conclusion. As far as I can remember now, I did not actually trace out this dissociated stream of thought at the time, but only knew that something of the kind must have happened."

In both these little episodes the introspective observer could recognize what had happened. But he might not have done so. In my own case, if I were one sort of person, I might have been eager to ascribe my intuitional diagnosis to the operation of a familiar spirit. The importance of the examples is in the fact that they show how the unconscious (or the sub-conscious, or the dissociated stream) *perceives and makes deductions on its own.* This possibility must be considered in every supposed case of thought-reading.

WATER-DIVINING

It is probable that in any gathering of ordinary people there will be some who have always taken for granted that water-divining is a generally accepted means of ascertaining the whereabouts of underground supplies. Then two possible opinions may emerge; some will express surprise if told that scientific men do not believe in it, whilst others will accuse scientific men of neglecting to enquire into and find a physical explanation of the mysterious power possessed by a few gifted people.

The supposed gift has, as a matter of fact, been critically investigated again and again and found to fail under test conditions. As usually employed, the test is always fallacious inasmuch as, if a well is sunk at the spot indicated by the dowser and water is found, there has been no control experiment; that is, to make it a real test, a well should be sunk where the dowser says water will not be found. I saw that check practically applied when a laundry was being built in the London area and the directors brought down a dowser from the North of England to tell them where to sink their well. He indicated a spot where it should be sunk but the manager-to-be of the laundry was perturbed because he had already planned his buildings and wanted the well next his engine-house. He mentioned his difficulty to me and, having an elementary knowledge of London geology, I ventured to tell him that it probably wouldn't matter in the least where the well was sunk. Eventually the common-sense course was adopted of asking the advice of the firm that would do the well-sinking, and my friend was gratified when told he could have it where he liked. Yet if the dowser's location had been adopted the finding of water would have been accredited to him as a success.

The affinities of the divining rod appear when we collate the manifold claims that are or have been made for it. It not only locates water, but oil, coal and other minerals; also buried treasure and dead bodies—it is not so many years since I read a serious account in a newspaper of how the police used a diviner in the attempt to locate the position of a corpse in a river. Janet, who studied it among what he called psychological automatisms, described its use in old France to follow the track of criminals, and this points to a connection with the witch-finding of primitive Africans, who used a stick that pointed to the victim. In the days when a gold sovereign was not such a rarity as it is now there were people who claimed to be able to use the rod to find one hidden under the carpet of a room. Sometimes it is claimed that the twig moves upwards to indicate water and downwards to indicate something else.

If we examine the working of the rod it turns out to depend upon an interesting mechanism. A hazel twig is the traditional choice, and this is determined by its toughness, springiness, and freedom from prickles, though I have seen quite a good show produced with a twig casually broken from a privet bush. The twig must be forked, the limbs of the fork being conveniently about eight to twelve inches long. With the apex pointing away from him the operator places the thumb and little finger of each hand inside the corresponding limb of the twig, his palms facing each other. Closing his fingers he now has the twig grasped firmly, but nothing much can happen until, with elbows close to his sides, he turns his knuckles outward and downward. Each limb of the twig is now forcibly bent and a trigger action tends to take place. By pressing the ring fingers against the twig the spring of the trigger is brought into activity and, if you are the experimenter and are not careful, the twig may suddenly rise and hit you in the face. With a little attention, however, you can make the twig rise gradually whilst you bend your hands down and persuade the bystanders, or even yourself, that you are doing your best to prevent it from rising. With practice you can press the ring fingers in the opposite direction and produce a downward instead of an upward movement of the twig.

It is plain that, having mastered this mechanism, you could now walk across, say, an underground stream whose existence is known to you, and make the twig rise at the proper place. You have become a dowser except that you know what you are doing and how you are doing it. But there are intelligent and honest people who would go through the same performance and declare they did not know what they were doing, and that the twig was moving itself; they might even deny that they had any knowledge of the existence of the water. Add all the other manifestations claimed for the divining rod, assume that the performers are in every case honest and intelligent, and that sometimes they turn out to be right, and we are faced with two possible explanations. Either there is a world of mysterious forces, unknown to science, which make the twig

rise or fall in many varied circumstances, or we are in presence
of a dissociation of consciousness. In the case of the water-
diviner the dissociated stream would contain:

 a. The control of the muscles making the twig rise.
 b. The mental processes involved in judging when
     water is present.

There is yet another factor that must be considered. We
have agreed that the dissociated stream perceives and makes
deductions on its own, and, closely akin to the thought-reading
I have just described, there is an alertness to pick up indications
from any source, whether from the physical surroundings or
from the behaviour of bystanders. A dowser whom I saw
tested over ground where he claimed to locate the position of
water-pipes was obviously picking up indications from the
bystanders, most of whom knew the whereabouts of the pipes.
It is difficult to hide such indications when one is in the presence
of a skilled and dissociated thought-reader; but I succeeded in
simulating an expectation that he would find water in one spot
where it wasn't, and the twig moved up just as I hoped it
would.

His ability to pick up indications from bystanders I propose
to call *receptivity*. This ability is not my discovery. In a personal
communication from an oil magnate I learned that, having been
bothered by people who claimed the power of divining oil,
he at last agreed to a test. Oil was then put underground in
suitable containers and the diviners were invited to locate it;
but my informant would not allow to be present anyone who
had been concerned in the hiding of the oil; he would not
even be present himself, lest he might unwittingly betray its
whereabouts. In the result the diviners made rather fewer
successful hits than the laws of chance should have given them.

It is not easy to avoid the suspicion that, in giving this
explanation of dowsing, I am making charges of fraud. The
same difficulty occurs often enough in those psychoneuroses
which may have been regarded as examples of organic disease;
if the psychiatrist declares there is no organic disease he is
likely to be accused of maligning an innocent sufferer. Here,
too, if I deny an external force for the movement of the twig

I am maligning the diviner. Of late years there seems to be an inclination to accept the movement of the twig as produced by the muscles of the diviner, but the muscles are now said to be influenced by the mysterious force, so we are not much nearer the truth.

I am not ready to assert that no diviner ever knows what he is doing and why he is doing it when he makes the twig go up; indeed, I should be surprised if this never happens. I am satisfied that in some examples known to me personally the diviner honestly believes that something external to himself makes the twig move. In the case of the water-pipes I thought the man was honest, though I was the only member of the party who did not accept his performance as evidence of the workings of an unknown mysterious force.

The belief in water-divining is an interesting survival in our scientific age. Its origin is unknown, though I have been assured that Moses, when he smote the rock with his rod and brought forth water, was the first to practise the art. At some times and places it may have been useful before the coming of geology, for the man with experience, especially one born and bred in a district and perhaps possessing lore handed on from father to son, would have a shrewd idea of where water would be found. The art still flourishes in the Cotswolds, where water supply is often a problem, and the business sign of the diviner is still to be seen.

I have been told, on good authority, of old countrymen who scorned the use of the twig but whose local knowledge and experience made their advice acceptable when wells were to be sunk. On such a basis I can grant the building up of a dissociation that, in similar circumstances, would have as much practical value as the conscious use of experience. Anything more I regard as a manifestation of credulity and of desire for the marvellous, with, on the part of the dowser, a dissociation that enables him to ignore his own mental processes.

MEDIUMISM

There has been no boom in spiritualism this time such as there was after the end of the first Great War, when there had

D

come down from the nineteenth century a rich development of its manifestations. Clairvoyance, table-turning, planchette, levitation, spirit controls, poltergeists, crystal-gazing, all had had their turn, and at the end of the war the writings of a famous physicist were acclaimed by many people as an authoritative confirmation of spirit revelation. This interest died down, though of course there were partial revivals, and one hears little of the subject now except that astrological forecasting seems to have some popular appeal.

There is no doubt that conscious and elaborate trickery has played a great part in the manifestations of mediumism, but its mechanical adjuncts are often like the diviner's twig in giving the opportunity for a dissociated stream to express itself. Planchette, which is a light platform on wheels, bearing a pencil, is an unstable affair almost impossible to keep still if two people rest their fingers upon it; with practice something like intelligible script can be produced. The table-turning performance, like planchette, is carried out simultaneously by more than one person, with the result that when the table moves no one knows who is moving it—not even the one who is actually doing so.

Divination by the swinging of a pendulum goes back to the time of ancient Rome and is also under the witting or unwitting control of the operator. Crystal-gazing is another inheritance from ancient days, and, like the trance state, may be a means of conscious trickery or serve the purpose of a dissociation. I have actually seen what looked like divination develop spontaneously in a case where I was sure that trickery was absent:

"An ex-soldier suffering from a war psychoneurosis had the usual loss of memory for emotional war episodes. When told to close his eyes, picture himself in France and describe what he was doing, he passed into a 'hypnoidal state' and recapitulated his experiences with some emotion. Among them, however, he interpolated incidents, such as were in those days described as war atrocities, which I disbelieved. When told to sit up and talk about what he had described he at once admitted that these incidents were not true but that they 'came into his mind.' At a later sitting he drifted on to talk about his service in India and once more produced obvious phantasies. He was uneducated but not lacking in intelligence and seemed puzzled by what was happening. Finally, he produced the story of a recent murder, a corpse having been found though details were still unknown. These details he filled in so circumstantially that it would have been easy for a credulous person to believe he had some extra-sensory means of gaining the information. On this occasion I spent some time in making him analyse the phantasy and it proved to refer to matters that had deep personal interest for him and showed themselves under this curious disguise."

This incident should be considered in connexion with the argument, sometimes used in reply to the true statement that mediums frequently show symptoms of a hysterical kind, that both the hysteria and the mediumistic powers are manifestations of a mental state that differs from the normal and is necessary for the development of those powers. This man, if he had been better educated, might have accepted his abnormality as a "gift" and cultivated it, or allowed it to be cultivated, till it ended in the destruction of his honest self.

There is a curious phenomenon sometimes seen in the insane and called *folie à deux*, when one person develops delusions and induces another to accept them as reality. The originator has, of course, a firm and obvious belief in them and dominates the other victim accordingly. There is, however, never much doubt as to the state of affairs, for the delusions are plainly to be recognized by any observer. But suppose the delusions are not so obvious, that there is already a tendency to believe them, and that the originator has unusual dominating qualities; there are then infinite possibilities of the spread of a belief in them. Except that the word *delusions* may not be correct, this supposition would fit the process by which Adolf Hitler achieved power in Germany.

With the same proviso we can apply this formula to the understanding of the poltergeist phenomena, which follow an extraordinarily uniform course. There is always concerned a young person with a reputation for innocence, with relatives who are so assured of that innocence that they accept all sorts of happenings as supernatural rather than question it. This puts the youngster in a dominating position which he or she fully exploits, and the relatives are made unwitting accomplices in the deceit. Then we have that human tendency to find satisfaction in personal association with the occult, together with a reluctance to admit having been deceived. All sorts of things now happen, chiefly in the way of articles being thrown about by an unknown force, the story gets into the papers, investigators come along and do everything except make expert psychological examination of the chief performer, and then the matter fizzles out till the next time. The frequent recurrence of this performance suggests that there is a common psychological basis for it; the easy explanation of a desire for notoriety as the cause is unlikely and it is a pity that the pathological nature of this behaviour has not been explored.

Returning to the more commonplace doings of the medium who uses one of the stock adjuncts of the craft, we meet material trickery of the grossest kind that has been exposed again and again, other examples in which apologists have declared that trickery is only used when the genuine medium fails to produce manifestations, and some in which the honesty of the performer seems undoubted. Of the last I have only seen one in which, although I was not present at the actual performance, the results of automatic writing were available to me and I was satisfied as to their genuineness. I do not infer, when I say that, that the product was to be accepted at its face value as a spirit revelation, but that the writer, like the honest water-diviner, really believed it to be the manifestation of some power outside himself. He had a dissociated stream of consciousness in which were memories derived from the reading of books, to which were added phantasies that built up a story of ancient Egypt as revealed by the spirit of a priest of those days. So convincing was he that at least two educated and intelligent men accepted the story and were willing to go to Egypt to conduct explorations with it as a guide.

Another example was *The Gate of Remembrance*, a book written about 1919 by F. B. Boyd, an archæologist who, with a colleague, had studied all the sources of information about a part of Glastonbury Abbey whose site was undetermined. Then they set out deliberately to produce a dissociation by means of automatic writing: As F. B. Boyd put it: "What was clear enough was the need for somehow switching off the mere logical machinery of the brain which is for ever at work combining the more superficial and obvious things written on the pages of memory, and by its dominant activity excluding that which a more contemplative element in the mind would seek to revive from the half-obliterated traces below."

Automatic writing was the means used to switch off the main stream of consciousness and produce a dissociation. It was apparently controlled by personifications of departed priests, but the writer was willing to accept them as vivid imaginary pictures and to credit to his own unconscious such passages as seemed to be helpful in further research. In my opinion the experiment was psychologically sound and intellectually honest.

I have tried to indicate the pitfalls that await us if we cling to the old assumption that every person not insane knows what he is doing and why and how he does it. If we accept this assumption it follows that for such doings as water-divining and mediumistic revelations the only possible explanations are conscious fraud or the existence of strange forces outside our ordinary knowledge and beyond the scope of science. The theory of the unconscious, aided in this field by the more limited theory of dissociation, avoids either assumption and gives us an alternative that brings them within the world of everyday life. This is, however, only a narrow application of such theories.

HYPNOTISM

The history of hypnotism shows some curious episodes in which public interest rises to a peak, strange and apparently wonderful things happen or are discovered, and mysterious forces are invoked to account for them. Then, somehow or other, discredit falls upon the manifestations and interest fades until the next revival. Yet serious investigators have steadily carried on with their experiments in spite of being regarded as cranks outside the realms of true science.

One of these episodes was the descent of Mesmer upon Paris towards the end of the eighteenth century, with his theories of animal magnetism. Clothed in impressive garb, he used metallic appliances to produce strange performances in his subjects, and actually succeeded in removing some symptoms. It is highly probable, however, that he often produced them before their removal. At first he was taken seriously and an official enquiry confirmed his claims. Later on, a further enquiry condemned him as an impostor (chiefly because magnetism could be excluded as a physical cause of his results) and he fled from the city, leaving behind, however, the word *mesmerism* to perpetuate his memory to this day.

The modern view of Mesmer is that he was not a conscious impostor, that he believed in his theories and actually produced phenomena of psychological importance which, if properly investigated, would have advanced our knowledge. After his departure a few disciples carried on experiments in out-of-the-way places, and it is likely that there is a continuity of practice or tradition from his day to the present.

About the middle of the nineteenth century there came a revival in this country. Elliotson, a surgeon attached to one of the teaching hospitals in London, used hypnotism to produce insensibility in patients during operations, but met with such opposition that he was obliged to resign from his hospital post. This was not, however, merely opposition to new ideas. Hypnotism had become entangled with clairvoyance, fortune telling, odylic force, and other manifestations of the occult then enjoying a wide range of popularity; it still carried the old idea of "animal magnetism," and on this basis, Gregory, an Edinburgh professor of chemistry, wrote a book containing fantastic accounts of the results of seances which were enough to repel anyone with the least critical judgement. It happened, too, that at this period the use of chloroform, ether, and nitrous oxide gas for the production of anæsthesia was becoming accepted; hence, in any case, the use of hypnotism for anæsthesia would have been superseded because of the ease and certainty of the new methods. It is recorded that after Robert Liston had performed his first operation under ether anæsthesia at University College Hospital in 1846, he turned to the assembled company and exclaimed, "This Yankee dodge beats mesmerism hollow."

The most extraordinary episode of all, however, is often overlooked. When a student I heard of Charcot, a French neurologist, as an eminent teacher at the Salpêtrière hospital in Paris and the discoverer, or describer, of a diseased condition of bone known as "Charcot's joint." There was an occasional reference to his work on hypnotism and hysteria, but only on going back to his own writings and other literature of the period is the full story to be understood.

He described a set of symptoms to which he gave the name of *grande hysterie*; these followed a stereotyped yet dramatic course, with convulsions of characteristic pattern that could be induced by appropriate stimuli. He also studied hypnotism in association with hysteria and believed that commands given to a hypnotized patient would be inevitably carried out. For example, a young woman under hypnosis, when given a pistol, told it was loaded, and ordered to shoot someone, would carry out the command. Public demonstrations of these happenings were given and legislation was demanded to protect the public from the terrible dangers manifest in this newly discovered force. One incident, however, threw a light upon these dangers, when a subject who had carried out dreadful deeds under hypnosis was hypnotized again by students, after the master had departed, and commanded to undress, but came out of the hypnotic state instead of obeying. She was willing to shoot or stab. That was only play-acting; the audience knew it was, the operator knew it was, and there is no reason why the subject should not know as well. However deep the hypnosis, she trusted the operator not to put a live cartridge in the pistol; but to undress in front of a crowd of students was no play-acting to this modest young woman, in whom conventional prohibitions were too strong for the command to work.

Charcot had a strange belief in the therapeutic use of metals, by the application of which various symptoms could be removed or altered. This was curiously reminiscent of Mesmer, and in 1882 the *Lancet* had a series of articles from a Paris correspondent roundly condemning much of this work as a repetition of the methods and results of the animal magnetists of a century earlier. A pretty speculation appeared years later when evidence was adduced that Charcot's first patient to present the features of *grande hysterie* had been under the care, or the tuition, of one of the heirs of the Mesmer tradition, who had cultivated in her the same sort of symptoms that Mesmer himself had produced. This woman found her way to the Salpêtrière, where her symptoms were taken at their face value by Charcot and regarded as examples of a real disease. This disease he now reproduced in other subjects and so built up his *grande hysterie* —which, by the way, has never been seen since those days. Axel Munthe, in *The Story of San Michele*, tells of a country girl whom he tried to rescue from the Salpêtrière after she had been converted into a full-blown performer in Charcot's repertoire. Axel Munthe could tell a good story, but his account accords with what actually happened there.

Bernheim of Nancy now entered into controversy with Charcot and finally it became manifest that the symptoms he described, like the hypnotic manifestations with which they were so closely related, were suggested to his patients and then accepted by Charcot himself as genuine. Charcot must have given up many of these beliefs by the time Freud attended his clinic in 1894.

An interesting relic of his teaching survived in English medicine till recent years, and shows the connexion between hysteria and hypnotism. A patient with a hysterical paralysis of a limb, when examined by Charcot, would be found to be so anæsthetic on the paralysed limb that needles could be thrust through folds of the skin without causing any sensation of pain. A strange thing was that, until it was discovered in the individual by Charcot, the patient was unaware of the anæsthesia. This teaching was current in my student days, and I recall a physician who, after demonstrating such an anæsthesia, turned to the students and exclaimed, "You see, she didn't know it was there, she didn't know it was there." *Why* it should be there was not explained, but I accepted the phenomenon as an integral part of the disorder till, in the 1914–1918 War, I was confronted by many such cases and astonished myself by discovering that the anæsthesia did not exist unless I suggested it. A man, pricked on the paralysed limb and asked, "Can you feel that?"

might flinch the first time, but would answer "No" and not flinch again. My question implied that I expected him not to feel—or why should I ask? So he accepted my suggestion and became anæsthetic. A little experimenting showed me that I could determine the degree of anæsthesia and by suitable suggestions produce a loss of sensation to quite severe knocks on the shin bone, the man, with eyes closed, declaring he did not know I was touching him at all though the blow might shake the limb. On the other hand, if I varied my suggestion as I pricked him, and asked "What does that feel like?" the man would give any answer except "I don't feel it." Later on I discovered that I was not so original as I thought, for Babinski had forestalled me by several years.[1] The accounts of witchcraft show that loss of skin sensation was one of the signs sought by witch-hunters; here we see one of several links between hysteria, hypnotism and witchcraft.

After Charcot's time the serious study of hypnotism was left to a few isolated workers, but it still had a popular appeal, and stage shows of hypnotism were common; I have a recollection of one about 1889, in which volunteers from the audience did many funny things like getting drunk on water and singing songs they wouldn't have sung when sober; also half a dozen were skilfully grouped in statuesque poses that they maintained for several minutes—so immobile were they that I suspect they were trained subjects planted among the audience. The study of the subject had little contact with medicine, though a few medical men found it of use in removing symptoms that they recognized as psychological. The war, however, brought a partial revival when many thousands of soldiers suffered from psychoneuroses—shell-shock and the like. Even then little was done by direct removal of symptoms under hypnosis. As I showed in the previous chapter, most of these patients had suppressed the memory of important emotional incidents, generally of a terrifying kind, and some psychotherapists found

---

[1] We have an exaggerated idea as to the pain caused by a fairly sharp needle or pin. I have known schoolboys to amuse their friends by thrusting a pin up to the head, in the fleshy part of the thigh, and on one occasion when I received a cut on the leg I stitched it up myself without feeling heroic. Yet the application of a painfully strong electric brush will overcome most hysterical anæsthesias.

D*

that the induction of a hypnotic state enabled them to revive these memories. It was at this time that I came in touch with the subject and it is perhaps due to something in my make-up that I could make little headway with direct hypnosis. Indeed, the only results I obtained were with men who were so distraught that sleep had become difficult. They responded quickly to hypnotic methods of inducing sleep.

Yet the simple method of revival described on pages 78 and 83 sometimes brought about conditions almost identical with hypnosis, though called by another name—hypnoidal. The man, though responsive to my voice, became oblivious of his surroundings and lived through his war experience as if again on the battlefield. Sometimes when I roused him by a simple command such as, "Sit up now," he might show difficulty in opening his eyes and appear bewildered at finding where he was. He might at once or a few days later deny all knowledge of what he had told me, though later on suitable technique was developed which could safeguard against this waste of labour and keep the revived memory in the normal consciousness. The man's state was a dissociation of consciousness and, though it is still convenient to call such a state hypnoidal, there is little difference between it and hypnosis. If one had cared to play tricks with the patient the stock manifestations of hypnotism could easily have been produced.

The situation after the war was that among psychotherapists —who were still to some extent outside the pale of medical orthodoxy—the methods of revival of memories and the detailed procedure of psychoanalysis had destroyed the individual doctor's reliance upon the healing power of hypnosis as such, and left it as a mere adjunct to revival.[1] Some readers, however, may remember the vogue enjoyed for a while after the war by M. Coué, with his suggestion of "Every day and in every way I get better and better." He also used the old technique of suggesting that a subject could not undo his clasped hands, and

---

[1] As noted in an earlier chapter, it is now usual to inject a drug to facilitate the revival of memories. Those who make of this a routine are often unaware of the ease with which many patients respond at once to the older and simpler methods. The use of a drug has received a ready approval very different from the scorn that nearly overwhelmed the work of the pioneers of revival by purely psychological technique.

some fell for that. His temporary success in public esteem was, I think, due to his being taken up by the opponents of psycho-analysis, for he was a nice old gentleman who said nothing about sex.

The results of hypnotic treatment have always been known as haphazard and evanescent, and now psychological know-ledge tells us why that is so. To remove symptoms by hypnotism is like chopping off the leaves of the dandelions on the lawn. Yet one must admit that sometimes the removal of the symptom may break a vicious circle and enable the patient to carry on happily. I once talked with a medical man who had been cured of a stammer by hypnotic treatment, and the operator had shrewdly advised him never to read anything about psychology, but to rest content with his cure. That operator was the most efficient hypnotist in London; he also knew that a knowledge of the psychological processes underlying a stammer might destroy the patient's belief that he was cured.

Because of our increasing knowledge of causes of nervous disorder it is unlikely there will in the future be much scope for the curative use of hypnotism, though there is little or no opposition to its use by any who may like to try it. To the public, however, it still has the appeal of the mysterious, and that appeal itself is powerful in making easy the induction of a hypnotic state in the individual.

SUGGESTIBILITY

This history of hypnotism shows how it is closely linked with the manifestations of hysteria. The latter is, by our defini-tion, a dissociation, with the dissociated stream of memories, emotions, and aims, existing alongside the main stream and sometimes taking its place, as in somnambulisms and fugues.

The hypnotic state is likewise usefully studied as a dis-sociation, the ordinary stream of consciousness being in abey-ance. The hypnotic stream is accessible to the hypnotist, receives his commands, accepts some of his statements unquestioningly, and is still in existence after the main stream of consciousness returns.

Because the hypnotic stream is accessible to the hypnotist

(a situation described as being *en rapport*) and critical powers are suspended, the hypnotic state is one of great suggestibility. That is easy to understand, but that the induction of that state should depend upon suggestion is another matter.

Such assumptions as magnetic power, the hypnotic eye, and other mysterious forces, have now given place to the "power of suggestion." That in turn has been elevated into a primary force, a kind of fairy petrol to be tapped by incantation, and we must try to form an idea as to what we mean by it.

McDougall defined suggestion as "a process of communication resulting in the acceptance with conviction of the communicated proposition in the absence of logical grounds for its acceptance."[1] At first sight this seems to separate off suggestion as an accidental intrusion into a logical world. The logical world, however, is a small one. Most of our religious, political and social beliefs, as soon as we examine them honestly, are seen to have arisen by any other process than logical reason, although it pleases us all to produce logical reasons for them if they are challenged. The belief comes first, before logical grounds are perceived, even if they can be found afterwards.

Trotter, who postulated a herd instinct as accountable for many elements in human behaviour, wrote, "Man is not, therefore, suggestible by fits and starts, not merely in panics and mobs, under hypnosis, and so forth, but always, everywhere, and under any circumstances."

As the member of a herd, man tends to think and feel as his fellows do; the fact that some idea is universally held is, indeed, occasionally put forth as evidence of its truth, but more often acceptance of the idea takes place without awareness of that reason.

Here we have one particular element in the success of suggestion at the start of any experiment in this sphere. Everyone has heard about hypnotism and shares in the belief that some influence outside the world of reason is at work. Many of us have heard how the assurance that a subject cannot separate his clasped hands produces an inability to do so. Let a personal friend try the experiment with us and the probability is that,

[1] *Social Psychology*, p. 97.

knowing him as just an ordinary fellow, we should smile at him and separate our hands. But let it be done in the raised expectancy of a public demonstration, by someone who has been extolled as a successful hypnotist, and some of us, already believing in what we think everyone knows, will fall for the suggestion.

This has its parallel in a condition that has been described among the natives of Malaya, called latah, in which the victim is impelled to imitate actions carried out by anyone who stands in front of him. A well-known illustration is of a man who had a baby in his arms when someone took up a lump of wood and pretended that was a baby, tossing it about and finally throwing it away, all these actions being imitated by the victim. This particular story may not be true, but the condition certainly has existed in a repeated and typical form and could only do so as long as people believed in its existence. Judging by what we know of hysterical suggestibility, one might expect it to be a symptom grafted upon an already existing psychoneurosis, for it is a more serious matter than the easy acceptance of one's inability to unclasp the hands.

The counterpart of the belief on the side of the subject is the belief in his own power, or technique, on the part of the operator. I have had long talks with one man of a humble walk in life who had discovered that he possessed "the influence." He believed in it and, according to his own account, had disconcerted the local practitioners by relieving people of symptoms they had failed to touch. Whether that were true or not, he certainly was full of confidence in his own ability to hypnotize and I saw no reason to doubt his success. Indeed, as I listened to him I realized that my own partial failure to hypnotize war-time patients probably arose from the fact that I had approached the subject with a willingness to try but an uncomfortable feeling that I was imposing upon the intelligence of my patient. I could go through all the usual formulæ, but a full emotional belief in their efficacy was lacking and my lack of self-assurance was probably sensed by the subject. On the other hand, to co-operate with an intelligent man in reviving his lost memories appealed to me as a straightforward and logical procedure, and I did not realize that I then possessed an assurance and self-confidence that were lacking in my attempts at hypnosis.

THE HYPNOTIC PROCEDURE

So far we have recognized as elements in hypnosis a belief on the part of the subject that hypnosis is possible—and, in the world as it is, the man who declares he cannot be hypnotized may nevertheless have that belief—and an equal belief on the part of the operator; but these elements do not account for the truly remarkable phenomena that regularly occur.

There have been different methods of inducing hypnosis; the use of "Mesmeric passes" has been given up and its place taken by various methods of tiring the eyes, such as asking the subject to look fixedly at an object so held as to make him turn his eyes upwards in a constrained position. When he showed signs of tiring the operator would push suggestions of a desire to close the eyes, invite him to let them close and then give assurance of feeling sleepy till at last the subject really fell asleep. Sometimes the operator dispenses with all aids except a comfortable position and relies entirely upon verbal suggestion. There is no one method, and every hypnotist probably has his own predilections. There seem, however, to be alternative principles at work, to command or to coax, and they may have some theoretical interest. Sleep may not come at the first attempt, but in a successful case the subject sooner or later falls into a sleep that at the start only differs from ordinary sleep inasmuch as he remains *en rapport* with the operator, hears his voice, and pays attention to him whilst continuing to sleep.

Now, it is possible to hypnotize not only credulous people and those ignorant of matters psychological. A trained psychologist has, in a personal communication, described how she was the subject in an experimental investigation and how, recognizing the impulse to carry out an action as being the result of a suggestion given her under hypnosis, she found herself so uncomfortable when resisting it that for her peace of mind she preferred to carry it out. I must add that she was, of course, a willing sharer in the experiment and she had a great respect for the eminent colleague who hypnotized her.

What parallel in the lives of all of us is there to this falling asleep under the influence of a voice? The answer is easy. The voice is the soothing or commanding voice of the parent, and the successful hypnotist is perhaps he who can recognize who will react more easily to one or the other.

In psychoanalysis there occurs the phenomenon of *transference*, a situation in which an emotion felt in the past, usually towards a parent, is revived in the analytical procedure and is directed upon the analyst, who then becomes the temporary recipient of trust and affection or of the reverse, hostility. The bringing into the present of a past emotion lying in the unconscious enables it to be worked through and, if need be, deprived of its harmful influence upon the adult patient.

We saw in a previous chapter that in all of us there lie the memories of infancy, sunk into the unconscious and yet active in their emotional influence. So in all of us there is the possibility of being hypnotized, of being put to sleep by the voice of someone who takes the place of the all-powerful parent, whether loved or feared, and receives, by a process of transference, the obedience due from the infant. This is the psychoanalytical theory of hypnotism. I do not know of any record of its being proved by the deep analysis of a subject who has been hypnotized in the past and has found out, in the course of analysis, the unconscious factors that influenced the hypnosis; but it should be possible to do this.

When this sleep is induced there ma be little difference from ordinary sleep and if left to himself the subject will eventually wake up as if from normal slumber. But ordinary sleep is a replacement of the conscious self by a dream self, a self that can in a dim way perceive stimuli and, not so dimly, experience emotion; the suspension of the stream of consciousness during sleep is followed by the coming into being of a dissociated stream. In hypnosis this dissociated stream is in contact with the hypnotist, and here arises the possibility of building up the "hypnotic personality" that has formed the basis of so much experimental work. Paradoxically, as this second personality is built up the resemblance to sleep diminishes till at last there is a fully conscious personality differing only artificially, I think, from the main personality. The new personality is *en rapport* with the hypnotist and, even when the main personality is restored, will carry out his orders *within the limits of the experiment*. If the subject is told that two hours after coming out of the hypnotic state he will stand on a chair he may do so, but, as in the case of Charcot's described a few pages before, he is not likely to do anything that would seriously violate his fundamental principles of behaviour.

AMNESIA AFTER HYPNOSIS

It may be suggested to the subject during hypnosis that he will not remember what has happened, but even without this suggestion there is often an amnesia, or loss of memory, for the events in the hypnotic state. I described how the man with amnesia for war episodes might recall them in a hypnoidal state but forget them immediately afterwards, and the victim of a fugue may wander for days before coming back to his normal self, when he may have no memory of his wanderings. The reader may understand this phenomenon if he has ever waked up from a striking dream, visualized it again, and later in the day failed completely to recall anything about it; such a process is as much an amnesia as any of the other phenomena here described and consideration of it will help in the realization that the loss of memory is not merely a subterfuge on the part of "an artful neurotic." The psychopathologist is often challenged as to the genuine nature of these amnesias. In any case the final proof of genuineness should rest upon the revival of the memory, when the behaviour of the patient easily indicates to the experienced observer that the revival is genuine. In the case of post-hypnotic amnesia, however, the revival is a much simpler matter for the hypnotist, who can often in a few words call into activity the cut-off stream of consciousness in which the memory is contained.

Hypnotism thus falls into place among other manifestations of dissociation of consciousness and should not be regarded as something possessed of mysterious or inexplicable qualities.

CHAPTER V

THE PSYCHOPATHOLOGY OF SEX

SEX INSTRUCTION

IF we accept the hypothesis that the foundations of a psychoneurosis are laid in the first few years of life, the question naturally arises whether any general principles of causation can be enunciated. The problem is not so closely related to ordinary education as might be supposed; it more closely concerns the emotional relationships within the family. Until recent years almost the only guidance was derived from the analysis of adults, but a technique of child analysis has now been developed which confirms and enlarges the experience already gained. The fact that the most common repressions concern sex lead us at once to the consideration of our attitude towards the young in regard to the subject, for it is against them that the sex taboo[1] is most strongly enforced. To prevent them from acquiring any knowledge of sex or reproduction is still the unspecified aim of many parents and educationalists, and there are those who would maintain the taboo indefinitely. Some would perpetuate savage custom and have a ceremonial removal of the taboo at a certain age, using, as textbooks of ritual, such publications as "What a Boy of Twelve should

[1] Taboo is a Polynesian word, first recorded by Captain Cook, who found that there were certain prohibitions to which this name was given. For example, if a hill were taboo, then no one must approach it for fear of some unknown, or at least unspecified, penalty. The taboo, though to all appearances irrational, was unquestioned.

Taboo in primitive peoples has been extensively studied by anthropologists who have, however, rarely dared to study our own taboos, being, like all of us, themselves subject to them. It occurs in most varied forms. A dead man's name may be taboo, and then any reference to him must be by some circumlocution; or a man's mother-in-law is taboo to him, and if the lady sees him approaching she must hide from him. Among the Trobriand Islanders Malinowski found a notable absence of taboos except that a man must know nothing about his sister's love affairs, nor admit their possible existence; but he noted that the equivalent of our smutty jest took the form of the violation of that taboo by some sly reference to the subject. Our own taboos are, curiously enough, strongest and most unquestionable in regard to words.

Know." Others discuss the advisability of having the information given by schoolteachers through the medium of lectures. All these suggestions imply some difficulty that is never clearly defined, and when we seek for definition we can find no difficulty intrinsic to the subject. If we ask what results would follow the complete lifting of the taboo we may meet with a cloud of rationalizations, extempore defences, that is, raised to guard our prejudices; vague suggestions of disaster will be made, and we shall find that some people anticipate an orgy of juvenile immorality unless ignorance is maintained. But sometimes it will be admitted that the parent feels unable, through inner inhibitions, to answer honestly and simply the inevitable questions of the child. The difficulty really lies in the adult attitude, and for that reason I am strongly opposed to any attempt to throw the onus of instruction upon teachers. In a case known to me, a young woman of twenty-four, victim of a washing mania that made life unbearable for her family, had been trained as a teacher and received lectures upon something called "physiology." She was completely inhibited upon the subject of sex and unable to refer to it except by the vaguest circumlocutions, but admitted that these lectures dealt with it. Since she could not talk about it I prevailed upon her to bring to me her notes of the lectures, where I found drawings representing uterus, Fallopian tubes and ovaries, fairly correct and properly labelled, no verbal taboos being involved, followed by the statements, "male organs visible externally," and "impregnation takes place by contact." This parody of instruction, acting upon a mind already prepared by the narrowest upbringing, had been sufficient to start the washing mania. When her inhibitions had been partially overcome she described the shamefaced manner in which the lecturer, a woman lecturing to women, had dealt with the subject, and the episode convinced me of the danger of entrusting any sex education of the young to people—parents, teachers, or physicians—still subject to the emotional inhibitions imposed upon them by our social inheritance.

Even among people who take active steps to advocate sex instruction there is a strong taboo still operative, and they are ready to adopt a circuitous route by way of teaching botany or letting the child keep rabbits, as if that sort of knowledge mattered. I once heard a lady declare, in a speech advocating sex instruction of the young, "In teaching children about these things we should not say *sex* but *gender*; *sex* is a nassty word."

Incidentally I might note that a textbook of physiology "for the use of schools," published not twenty years ago, made no reference to the reproductive organs and only very guardedly hints at the excretory functions. Whoever is responsible for such a production ought to be called upon to explain what he imagines to be taking place in the mind of the child who recognizes that these subjects are too dreadful or disgusting to be referred to by adults.

The problem does not exist on the part of the child until it has been manufactured by adult influence. When, however, the taboo has been recognized by the child and made a part of his mental equipment, the barrier thus created is strengthened till any attempt on the side of the adult to penetrate it is baffled. Before a parent sets out to impart to his child "what a boy of twelve should know," let him first try to find out what that boy of twelve already knows. He will find it impossible. I recall one lad of fourteen who was doing badly at a large boarding school and in whom I suspected that the usual adolescent troubles were at work. Seated by a fireside where a cat was purring, I asked him, "Interested in cats?" "Yes," he answered. Then I asked where kittens came from. "They come from inside the mother cat." "And where do babies come from?" "Oh, they come from heaven." This defence was impregnable at one interview, and one can only pity a boy upon whom such obstinate lying had been forced by our prejudices.

In another case, the mother of a lad of eighteen who suffered from symptoms that had made school life almost impossible told me that she had imparted some information about birth to him when he was aged twelve, but "he didn't seem the least bit interested." He had been a pupil on a farm for six months and assured me that all he knew about cattle breeding was that the bull and the cows were put in a field together and after a while the cows had calves. His symptoms demanded analytical treatment and when the barrier was broken down he poured out a stream of conscious sexual phantasies that had existed almost from infancy. There had existed the usual struggle against them, and the parents' belief in the boy's "innocence" had allowed them to expose him to stimuli which caused him great distress; he had, for example, been allowed, when on a holiday, to share a bed with a nurse who had already become the object of his phantasy, and the description of the mental state thus produced in him was pitiful.

The parental attitude in some cases is quite characteristic. The mother of the patient with a washing mania assured me that she had been "most carefully brought up"; so carefully had she been brought up that in the house special traffic regulations were made so that her grandfather should never be seen going to the water closet, he himself having inhibitions in that respect. Such regulations might have been harmless but for the emotional emphasis placed upon them. Knowing the family characteristics, I picture the mother laying down the regulations with lowered voice and sidelong glances expressive of a dreadful unknown. The effect of such an influence acting from earliest infancy was to induce a terrible dread of anything to do with such matters.

The mother of another patient who had starved herself to a skeleton, assured me that her daughter never, she was sure, gave any thought to such matters as the mystery of birth; when the mother had sought to give instruction to her fourteen-year-old girl she had been met with the protest, "Oh, I don't want to hear about such things." From that and other indications the conclusion was almost certain that the starvation in some way represented a fear of pregnancy, especially as the only other obvious symptom was an intense interest in women's dress—and not from the standpoint of pure fashion.

The question is not that of giving or not giving information. The ordinary child asks many questions that the ordinary adult cannot answer, or full answers may be so far beyond the comprehension of the child that they must be withheld; but when the inevitable questions about birth or sex are asked they are met in a special emotional manner. Not only is information refused, but the refusal implies at the best an irrational denial of the child's right to know and at the worst an emotional reaction on the part of the parent that invests the whole subject with mystery and dread. The reaction of the child varies according to the strength of the infantile complexes that seem to be always present in endless combinations. The foundation may be laid for fear reactions or morbid anxiety, for resentment towards authority as a permanent character trait, for obsessional speculation or, though this I have never verified, for scientific curiosity. I am inclined to think that the child comes off best who meets the situation on the conscious level, setting out to make his own discoveries from playmates, and celebrating them by cheerful indulgence in schoolboy obscenity. I have, on the other hand, known a reasonably informed girl to check fantastic speculation and impart decent instruction to her fellows in the dormitory of a boarding school, though perhaps at the risk of her own reputation if the matter had been discovered.

Prophylaxis as applied in this direction plainly involves the absence of emotional inhibitions on the part of the parent. If that state of affairs exists there is no problem, neither is there any need to pay special attention at all to the matter of instruction except so far as it becomes necessary to warn the child of the presence of the taboo. With confidence once established the child may be frankly told that there are people who regard it as wrong that he should know of such matters and that he must mould his behaviour accordingly. The amount of conscious hypocrisy involved in this attitude is harmless in comparison with the results of the traditional method, which enforced not only hypocrisy and lying, but pathological suppression with all its disastrous results. If the child knows he is free to ask questions and have them answered unemotionally we can afford to neglect his state of knowledge and need take no steps whatever in the direction of "sex instruction." If we make him feel that the subject is invested with some mysterious and dreadful quality, all efforts at instruction will be worse than useless.

Akin to this problem is that of masturbation, and here we find an even greater display of emotional reaction on the part of the adult. If we were frank we should discover that masturbation is so common as to fall into place as a stage in sex development. Although there is a mass of deeply entrenched superstition, dating from the time of Tissot in the eighteenth century, which ascribes innumerable maladies to this habit, yet there is no evidence of any physical ill-effects caused by it. It was once the custom to talk of dementia præcox as "masturbatory insanity," because open and shameless masturbation is sometimes an early symptom, but the widespread belief that the latter causes mental disease is without foundation. Mental distress of the acutest kind it certainly does cause, partly on account of its becoming linked up with the sex taboo or associated with deeper complexes, but chiefly because the false teaching as to direful results—teaching carried on alike by well-meaning mentors and unscrupulous quacks—is accepted and made a source of conscious fears. Towards the end of the first World War it happened more than once that when I sought to ease the mind of some "war neurasthenic" by assuring him that his troubles were not a result of early masturbation, I was confronted with a brochure issued by some "League," repeating luridly the worst superstitions about its supposed evils. Treatment of the nervous condition was impossible until all belief in the statements of the brochure had been destroyed.

Those experiences, however, are insignificant beside the sufferings of the child who has been discovered to be—say it with bated breath—a masturbator. He is watched, questioned in an awe-inspiring manner as to repetitions of his sin, perhaps has his hands tied at night, and is made to feel an overpowering sense of guilt. Medical textbooks used to describe the signs to be seen in the masturbating child, but all the appearances are those of shame and guilt; the child lucky enough to escape those feelings shows no signs and suffers no ills.

If we take this view we shall save a great deal of suffering, but it must be admitted that masturbation may be itself an indication of something amiss. The solitary child may masturbate because he is solitary, and he may be solitary not from lack of companions but from temperamental difficulties. The child whose outlets of affection are blocked may drift towards narcissism by the route indicated by a patient who, under analysis, described his early masturbation—which was carried into adult life and interfered with his marital relations—as "I enjoyed myself with myself and by myself." His difficulty was not the masturbation but the more deeply-rooted inability to feel affection for anyone; when rebuffed by a stepmother the child would deliberately retire to masturbate, and found in the act a substitute for the affection he could at that time have received and returned.

In another case a girl of twelve was brought to me because she was unable to learn. There was no lack of intelligence and after I gained her confidence she volunteered that her trouble was masturbation. But, to my surprise, she went on to say that it was not the masturbation itself—"I only do it when I am nervy," were the poor child's own words—but the constant watching of her mother, who never allowed her to be alone for a moment if she could prevent it, and even stood outside the water closet whilst the girl was within. I was roundly abused when I urged the mother to ignore the masturbation and give up her watchfulness, and had no opportunity of following the progress of the case.

CHANGES NOW TAKING PLACE

When ladies' legs were unmentionable and invisible, any allusion to them conveyed a dash of spiciness inconceivable to our youths and maidens, who view knees, like noses, with equanimity. The younger generation seem to have taken things in hand for themselves, and there is a freedom of social relations between the sexes that has become accepted by those whose Victorian traditions might still be expected to take offence. The middle-aged even seem loth to recall the days when seaside authorities posted up regulations telling where women were allowed to bathe, in garments defined as "from neck to knee," whilst their male friends and relatives were permitted to bathe only at a most respectful distance in garments which were publicly defined as "avoiding exposure of the person." These taboo-ridden prudes were horribly indecent.

In spite of the remaining taboo upon nakedness, nudist camps exist where, I am credibly informed, children and adolescents accept the situation without embarrassment and even discuss quite freely how far it is necessary for them to conceal their participation when they return to ordinary life.

SOME RESULTS OF THE SEX TABOO

Few people now react violently towards the idea that the psychoneuroses have most often a basis somewhere in the emotional side of sex life, though equally few would agree with Ernest Jones when he said they were "only a part of the price that society pays for its hypocrisy and its moral and intellectual obliquity." How does this come about? To begin with, the child is brought up to set the emotional, irrational and authoritative above the understandable and logical.[1] This is far from the conscious acceptance of custom, convention or moral principles, though unfortunately the taboo is often regarded as identical with morality. If a child by chance uses a forbidden word it is necessary, for his own happiness, that he should learn it is one of the things that aren't done. I know from my own experience that this lesson can be easily given and accepted without emotion. If the child asks why the word is prohibited —and a well-brought-up child should ask—he or she can be told the plain truth; there is really nothing the matter with the word, but people think it shouldn't be used. I remember one child who retorted with, "Well, I think that's silly."[2] I agreed with her, and was gratified to overhear her putting another child right with regard to the same word, and with the same explanation. If, as is more usual, the child is emotionally reprimanded, the word is falsely invested with a moral significance that may result in a defiant use of it or a feeling of apprehension when it is heard. I have known a patient who, among other obsessional symptoms, had a compulsion to repeat this particular word to herself and was much comforted by a discussion of the different etymological explanations suggested for its tabooed employment.

From the emotional and pseudo-moral emphasis upon the

[1] It seems a far cry from this to the subservience of the German people to Adolf Hitler, but was not his success due to their readiness to behave in accordance with such upbringing? Look round the world to-day and one will see that the emotional, irrational, and authoritative appeal defeats on almost every occasion the understandable and logical.

[2] The word was *bloody*, used in its correct sense, which is taboo here but not in America, where a reporter would write of a *bloody* knife when his English opposite number would say *blood-stained*. Bernard Shaw popularized the word, but even now it cannot be used with its primary meaning.

sex taboo there results the conception of a mysterious and dreadful world, to which the child is attracted by natural curiosity. The tough-minded boy gets over the difficulty by a course of schoolboy smutty talk; the tender-minded and over-scrupulous cannot do that. If the adult psychoneurotic is asked, "How did you get on when your schoolfellows talked smut?" he may reply, "I never could join them in it," or, "I always felt the odd man out." What is of still worse omen, he may deny that they ever did talk it, which signifies either an amnesia, or that he was treated by them as a prude and an outsider, not to be admitted to the secrets of the initiated. Such replies are a commonplace from those who reach the consulting-room of the specialist.

Girls behave differently, and either remain in ignorance or discuss the subject seriously. The following episode is instructive:

"The head-mistress of a girls' school came for my advice after her discovery of a secret society in the school, properly organized with officers and a minute-book and devoted to the study of the forbidden subject. She produced an essay on pregnancy and parturition which she admitted to be better than anything the writer did in school, though some of the phraseology shocked her. I pointed out that the girl had to use such words as were available to convey the sense, that there was no seeking after the obscene, and advised her to call a meeting of the society and tell them that if they wanted to know any more she would oblige. After saying she would have to get the parents' consent she decided to try the experiment. A few days later she rang me up to say the meeting had taken place with no more embarrassment than a tea party and the girls seemed quite happy about it. Then later on came a painful sequel. The parents of the writer of the essay had given the girl a beating, and what could she do about it? I advised that the parents, the two of them, should bring the girl to me, which they did. The parents were the ones needing treatment, and the father, who had done the beating, assured me that if he didn't do something about it his daughter 'might become a prostitute.' I think I was able to be polite whilst I told him, truthfully, of the disasters that might follow from his action."

Returning to the fate of the tender-minded of either sex, we find that the simplest and most straightforward ill effect is the production of anxiety symptoms. Whatever curiosity, knowledge, phantasy or desire has ever existed is repressed and passes out of conscious control; but the fear associated with it is also out of control, and rises into consciousness, though its cause is unknown. Fear cannot exist without an object, so it is projected on something external and appears as pathological anxiety.

Guilt is, of course, associated with the struggle to suppress and itself rises into consciousness and plays a great part in nervous symptoms and inhibitions.

It must be recognized that the taboo, usually regarded as keeping the child or adolescent from an interest in sex, paradoxically acts in precisely the opposite direction, even when all conscious interest seems to be banished.

Here is an example in which the continued suppression of sexual references stimulated the recognition of them:

"A lady in the early thirties complained of recurrent inexplicable 'panics.' She had been brought up in the old-fashioned way and shunned any reference to things sexual. The memories of a few isolated incidents had been suppressed and when these were brought into consciousness and freely discussed her inhibitions were lessened as far as the analytical procedure was concerned. Some early panics were then brought into the scope of the analysis and proved to be linked up with these memories, a chance incident in each case having stirred up the emotion associated with one or other of them. This reaction had then been intensified till at last anything capable of a sexual *double entendre* could produce a panic. On one occasion the lady had set out to tell an innocuous story she had heard on the wireless but had suddenly been seized with a panic and was unable to complete it. When made to recapitulate the story at the analytical session she suddenly cried out, 'What a fool I was,' and was able to explain the *double entendre*, which was of schoolboy simplicity. As time went on she learnt to recognize these tricks of her unconscious and detect the sexual meaning it attached to non-sexual subjects, and finally, when sex had lost its abnormal emphasis, the *double entendre* ceased to obtrude itself."

In an earlier chapter the connexion between the germinal sex instinct of the infant and its emotional relations to the parents was touched upon. It is this part of psychoanalytical findings that is most difficult of acceptance, and it is still regarded as a matter of deduction rather than observation. By the kindness of a colleague I am able to give an unusual example of such findings, for it was produced in the course of a self-analysis such as very few people are capable of. The patient had made a start with analysis but circumstances cut it short and she decided to carry on by writing out her own associations rather, but not entirely, in the manner of automatic writing, with an occasional visit to her analyst. Her complaint had been of an entire absence of feeling, or of emotional contact with people, so that the whole world seemed unreal. It emerged that the absence of feeling was primarily an absence of sex feeling; indeed, aversion had taken its place and even to be touched by another person was repugnant to her. Because of this a tentative love affair was broken off almost as soon as it had begun. The script here produced, only one chapter in a long story, was preceded by a dream in which, among other items, she felt herself to be pleasantly swathed in swansdown:

"In going back to the time when the swansdown-warmth and lightness was a sensation to me, as a baby, I had gone back to the time before I had learnt that feeling could be wicked, because as well as the physical pleasure there was in being wrapped in swansdown I felt that it was happening in my mind as well, and there was no case for an argument as to whether or not I should have that nice feeling in my mind. It was just life, when one's mind and one's sensations of pleasure are all one.

"Then I was aware of Miss —— and my mother in my life, and they arrived like a frost on the scene, and the warmth in my mind was frozen up.

"Then I saw B—— [her would-be lover] come into the garden and bring sex with him.

"I understand my dream better.

"When I was afraid of the farmer's scorn of the snake in the grass idea, and also my own awareness of the simplicity of the idea, I was aware of myself as the garden, and its sexlessness, and that B—— would not allow it to remain like that. When he came into the garden he brought sex with him. Although it has not been accepted in every corner of the garden yet it will be.

"It becomes acceptable when I see such pictures in my own mind as the swansdown one. It seems that from that I accept a small part of what it meant to enter the garden.

"Now, I do not know what Miss —— [a prudish nanny] and my mother really meant. They plainly brought something that banished the acceptance of sensation in my mind. But what part of life are they? I would like to see them as no part at all.

"It seems as though they have made me too much afraid to dare to allow my sensations to be a part of my mind.

"These things are not so much thoughts as actual happenings in my mind. The effect of Miss —— and my mother is so real that it seems as though there is a real and actual blanket on my mind that is moving, as I question my own feelings about sensation.

"Feeling-sensation, refers to sex, from earliest babyhood. The pleasure of the baby at its mother's breast is the same feeling of well-being in sex feelings. One has only one lot of pleasure feelings. They cannot be divided into the charming feelings of the baby, and the hush-hush sensations in sex which was part of the idea about feeling I gathered from Miss ——.

"Sensation became blighted because I found that it embraced sex, and that there was no limiting or binding of feelings. They are there, and one must either acknowledge, and accept them or refuse them, as I have done, when they only continue to exist and give trouble."

[Later] "I know that once I had the swansdown feeling, and that it has since disappeared. I have traced most of that loss to Miss —— and my mother, and I have seen that their views were backed up by my father.

"My feeling about Miss —— and my mother is a mixture of anger and understanding. But my feeling to my father is just anger, because he understood well enough to prevent my loss of feeling, and he did not do it.

"I feel towards him, as a child feels who has some treasure taken away from it—baffled, and enraged. If he had allowed it to, that swansdown idea could have continued; as it was, it became something horrid.

"I did not want that feeling to be concerned, except in passing, with my father. It was only the baby's feeling then, and I did not expect it to continue as that, through my life, but my fury with my father's attitude made that happen. It is too small a feeling to encompass all that I am putting into it, and it means frustration.

"It seems to me, that if he had understood and acknowledged my sensation feelings, I should have done so myself, passed through them there, and they would have grown up with me and been a useful receptacle for the feelings that came as I grew up.

"Other feelings did come as I grew up, and they all went to that same spot, and meant the same thing. By ignoring those feelings, when they had centred on him, he made me feel very wretched, and everything that touched on those feelings, from that day to this, has also been wretched.

"I don't think those sensations, swansdown feelings, are the same as the serious sex feelings of the baby to her father. They were an interesting and pleasurable experience that occurred on my way through life, and not an attempt to steal into the grown-ups' world, they were my feelings, as a baby only, but they could not be scorned, because that did them harm.

"What is the meaning of touch, just ordinary touch, in all this?

"I could not acknowledge touch before, now it means something, and it is allied to the swansdown feeling.

"Touch is connected with B—— bringing sex into the garden, and the wretched feelings of the baby.

"Earlier in this work I hated the thought of being touched, now it seems in some way symbolic of feeling. It seems to express in physical form, what is in my mind emotionally. I hardly realized that skin sensations meant so much.

"The difference in touch now is, that I see it as a pleasurable expression of some feeling in my mind. I can see also that there were horrible, miserable feelings in my mind, and that physical touch, touched them.

"There is a connexion, even a link, between the horrid idea of touch and the pleasurable idea, and that is something that seems more real to me.

"I dislike the link in many ways, but because it really feels a part of me, it is reality, and therefore welcome.

"It takes me to the time when I was about thirteen, and decided not to feel, or really just before the necessity not to feel, came about.

"It seems as though something actually took place in my mind.

"First, I was untroubled by any disturbances in feeling. In fact, the idea that one could think about feeling at all, had not occurred to me. Then something alien and horrible came into my mind, that I wanted to push out of it at once, but I could not do so, so long as I thought about it, and I found that if I was aware of feeling that gave power and importance to this alien, horrible thing, so I had to pretend there was no such thing as feeling.

"The alien thing is rather like a huge, painted, wooden image, like the Red Indians had, they were either Gods or Devils that they worshipped or feared. It did not seem to be a real human being for whom one had real, human feelings, but it did demand that one had human feelings for it. It demanded a human sacrifice in the form of human feelings to it, the whole time. It consumed one's feelings and gave nothing back.

"This wooden image stood for something, but I do not know what."

[Later] "This wooden image, consuming my feelings, was a description of what was happening to my sex emotions.

"In the frustration I felt about my father's scorning of my infantile sensations, there was nothing of the superstitious feeling that there is in the wooden image, and which is one of its strongest and most disturbing qualities.

"I suppose the idea in a wooden image is that it represents the God of one's tribe for generations without number, that it has the power to impart good or evil, and one is afraid of it and placates it, at all times.

"The idea that anyone could question the right to such power of these Gods is almost unthinkable, but it seems as though that is what I have been doing, without knowing it, and I have found out that the roots are rotten. In fact, I have found out that they have roots, and are not quite such Gods.

"It is the power of the grown-up world that the wooden Gods represent, and I resent it. I do not resent their experience as grown-ups, but the way in which they used it against me."

[Later] "It seems to me that I have found out why the grown-up world found it necessary to put certain Gods into the minds of children, but I have not been able to reduce their God-like authority.

"These Gods were put in charge of sex feelings—so sex feelings became inaccessible, and I cannot realize that they are ordinary human feelings.

"I do not know whether it is possible to take the Gods to pieces, so that they no longer exist, or whether one realizes that sex feelings are human, and dispose of the Gods that way.

"I think it is necessary to dispose of the Gods first.

"They came into existence in my mind by reason of the taboos Miss —— put on to nakedness, and interest in a human body, my own, as a child, but more particularly—the grown-up body. With that interest, there is a sense of well-being, and something like the swansdown sensation feeling.

"To set up a God to prevent one's interest in the body, was one thing, but that it should strike fear into the sensation part of that, was much worse.

"I felt that for me to think about sex feelings was wicked, that is, to think about them with the idea that I have sex feelings. Now I question that I feel as though I dare to think of them as mine, even though I do so rather fearfully, and the things that I question are found by groping in a black pit.

"These things are to be feared, I feel that they belong to the grown-up world. They are both fascinating and horrible, so that I feel I do not really want them. I feel like a child who has stolen into the grown-up world and who finds things fascinating but unmanageable.

"Has the grown-up world made sex life appear like that to me? I should hate any of those things to really belong to me, because I am afraid of them.

"The things I found were typical of Miss —— and my mother, and they made everything seem frightening so that I wanted to run away.

"I found two treasures in the pit. One was some soft black material, and the other was gold and glittering. The black material—like georgette—might have been the swansdown, in a happier world. The gold made it worth while to go into the pit, because I felt that all these treasures really belonged to me. But I was more afraid of the gold than anything, although the georgette made me feel miserable.

"It seems that I am aware of those two treasures, but I hate the feeling they give me and I try to escape from it."

[Later] "I do not think it is true to say that I cannot feel, but that I do not like what feeling means to me, as I see it in the black material and the gold.

"The arrival in my mind of those two things stops the rot that was spreading up the wooden images; and they add to the feeling of unreality.

"It seems as though the black material is touch—skin sensation, and the gold could be the sex act itself. But their presentation in this black pit is horrible.

"The idea of skin sensation was at one time abhorrent. It seems to me that it is the representation of it in my mind that is responsible for that, and the same is true of the sex act.

"The feeling about the black material and the gold is something like the feeling I have for the wooden images. I saw fear and awe in them, and also I hated having them in my mind."

[Later] "The black material and the gold were feelings I discovered. But they give me a horrible feeling. They feel slimy—the black does, and as though it is dragging me down into the pit all the time, and I hate the slimy feeling of the things that catch hold of me. The thought of the gold is not a question of feeling, I am in complete panic in case the slimy things pull me down into the pit, where the gold is. But it is possible to ignore the pull of the slimy things, so that the danger of falling into the pit is diminished.

"If I really allow myself to feel, I hand myself over to the slimy things in the pit, and from then I am in their power."

SEX ABERRATIONS

When I first picked up a now well-known book on sexual psychopathology it dealt with a strange world that to me, a medical man, was without relation to the one I was living in. As it happened, however, the subject was then beginning to be seriously studied, and that strange world has now become familiar. Havelock Ellis, whose early writings drew the active attention of the police, died in the odour of respectability. His works are now available for anyone wishing to study that world and there is no need for me to do more than give a very general survey of those psychological abnormalities that show themselves as sex aberrations.

The most distressing are psycho-sexual impotence in men and frigidity in women, which underlie much domestic unhappiness and have the most varied causes. They are generally capable of successful treatment.

More striking are the sex perversions (the word does not necessarily imply condemnation) which are far more common than is generally thought and whose nature is little understood even by those who are aware of their frequent occurrence. They may be described as a mis-direction of the sex impulse into abnormal channels and occur independently of the volition of the victim, who often would welcome their correction and may seek treatment for them if he knows that it is possible.

Homosexuality is perhaps the most important. Occurring in either sex, it has legal importance only in the male. It is sometimes claimed to be congenital but, apart from those rare cases of physical deformity in which the external organs of one sex are associated with the internal organs of the other, it is difficult to establish this, though the victims themselves often claim it is the case. Psychoanalysis enables it to be traced back to infantile reactions such as, roughly speaking, identification of the boy with his mother and the adoption of her

E

sexuality. Examples have been recorded of a mother, disappointed in the sex of a male child, bringing him up as a girl and so far succeeding as to make him a homosexual, and this confirms the likelihood of the psychoanalytical hypothesis, for what conscious effort can achieve can be achieved by unconscious influences. It is accepted that boys normally pass through a phase of homosexuality before reaching that of attraction to the opposite sex, and it is likely that arrest at that stage only takes place when earlier influences have already been at work.

The attitude of the male homosexual towards his abnormality varies enormously. One may be horrified when he discovers it in himself, another may accept it but carry on without ever seeking satisfaction for the impulse, another may give way to it with misgivings, another may seek every opportunity of satisfying it, whilst some glory in it and regard themselves as privileged above the herd. Perhaps the most instructive cases, as illustrating the complete replacement of the normal impulse by the abnormal, are those in which a love affair takes place with as much emotional emphasis as any heterosexual attachment.

There are as many kinds of homosexuals as there are heterosexuals. In the case of the latter we take a man's sexuality for granted before exercising judgement as to his sexual behaviour, and it would be well if we could adopt the same attitude before judging the former. To condemn the homosexual, as such, is ignorant prejudice. The following notes are from the case of a working man who sought help for his trouble:

"Is working with his father. Traces homosexual feelings back to the age of six or eight, but did not recognize their nature till sixteen. 'Females are nothing to me.' Fond of houses and furniture. Would like needlework but won't do it. Expresses the strength of his impulse by saying, 'I would have been a prostitute if I had been a woman.' Never mixes with men, but men give him a feeling of protection. 'I want a man to look after me as well as sexually.' Is drawn towards one man who has similar tastes, but has no knowledge of his sexual attitude. Dislikes to smoke in public. 'You could spot me a mile off for a woman smoking.' He asks for castration in the hope that it will remove all sex feelings."

This man gives a striking example of isolation; he has never made the acquaintance of another homosexual, whereas there is a strong tendency for these people to seek each other out and form coteries.

Cure is possible by analysis in but few cases. One may illustrate its difficulty by imagining a heterosexual in a homosexual community where his own impulses are condemned and punishable. As a matter of convenience he might be willing to be made homosexual by the waving of a magic wand, but in his heart he would have no desire for the change. So it is with the victim of the perversion, and he can rarely give that whole-hearted co-operation necessary for successful treatment: the psychotherapist has no magic wand.

Female homosexuality receives little attention except when a woman is found to be masquerading as a man, and sometimes even entering into a kind of marriage with one of her own sex. It is often latent; that is, it is n   recognized by the subject of it, who honestly regards herself as sexless till something calls up the hidden impulse. The same thing happens with the male, and accounts for some of those cases in which a man of unblemished reputation suddenly commits a serious offence that may surprise him as much as it does his friends.

Sadism and Masochism

These words, coined from the names of men whose perversions have received undeserved attention in literature, have been freely bandied about of late years. The germs of these aberrations lie in all of us, and I have more than once had the opportunity of noting the effect that publicity given to their manifestations has in stimulating a tendency towards either perversion. The victim of a sadistic or masochistic impulse may turn from that impulse in horror, or may gloat over any reference to it, and in either case publicity is an evil. That being so, I propose to avoid any discussion about corporal punishment in schools, except to say that incidents connected with it come up again and again in the history of patients whose sex instinct has followed some abnormal path.

FETISHISM

This curious but widespread aberration chiefly affects males and shows endless varieties. It is marked by the attraction of the sex impulse towards some inanimate object usually, but not always, connected with the opposite sex—shoes, corsets, hair, handkerchiefs, clothing, plastic raincoats, furs, artificial limbs, creaking leather, and so on. This list sounds ludicrous but is genuine.

The fetishism may be absolute; that is, only the fetish object is necessary for the full satisfaction of the impulse. Or it may be partial, when the article must be worn by someone who becomes the love object. Although the varieties of fetish are endless yet there is a curious repetition of stock patterns that are not the result of suggestion or initiation but arise independently in the individual. Here is an example of such a pattern in a man who believed himself to be the only one that ever experienced such an abnormality:

"Aged forty-four. Was always the baby boy. His mother held him back from school till seven. Not good at sports. Was called 'pussy' by the other boys. Has suffered from debility, and received various treatments for it, including spiritual healing. Been married eight years. Neither he nor wife is very amorous. Says intercourse is throwing strength away for no pleasure. 'Sex never attracted me. I dreaded it when courting.' The thought of intercourse is repulsive. Always had a mania for high-heeled shoes and corsets and a longing to wear them. Has bought them and put them on secretly with resulting pleasure. The sight of the print of a woman's heel on soft ground excites him terribly. Has dreams of wearing women's dress."

This shoe fetishism is perhaps the commonest, and is catered for in some quarters. I believe that the Chinese practice of foot-binding was a nation-wide cult of foot or shoe fetishism.

There is nothing to gain by further detail, but again we see that what may occur independently of volition, and therefore call for understanding rather than hasty condemnation, may be cultivated by those who rejoice in it. There are other abnormalities of sex behaviour to which the same considerations apply. To regard them simply as cases of wilful depravity is to remain ignorant, and ignorance in such matters is rarely profitable to society.

A DISEASE OF CIVILIZATION

These disorders are almost peculiar to civilization, and in them the strongest instinct in nature is diverted from its normal channel. We know that this does not originate in any conscious desire to take the abnormal path, however much the perversion may be cultivated when once it is established; it has its origin in unconscious mental processes. A few examples given in this book show the strength of the repressing forces that prevent sex ideas from being assimilated and check the even and natural development of the instinct. (Once again, repression does not mean control or restraint as applied to behaviour, but the thrusting down of something into the depths of the mind so that only indirect and distorted impulses or emotions can reach consciousness.) This powerful instinct being thus dammed back, it flows over into other channels and, through some concatenation of family emotions, follows the homosexual course; or, through a chance early association of some object and a sexually tinged emotion, it comes into consciousness as a fetishism; and, if neither of those perversions suits the occasion, many others are available. It used to be charged against psychoanalysis that it over-emphasized sex; there is nothing in psychoanalysis to approach the terrible emphasis placed upon sex in our traditional handling of the child. Perhaps that is a necessity of civilization, and sex perversion is a price worth paying for it; or is this emphasis the result of a taboo that we dare not destroy for fear of a dreadful unknown penalty?

It is an axiom of psychotherapy that when a child is brought for treatment it is the parent that needs it; but woe betide the psychotherapist who is too ready to say so. Looking back on the early opposition to psychoanalysis one recognizes the same situation; that the psychoneuroses were due to the imperfections of our social structure was a supposition not to be tolerated. We are now more ready to admit that sex abnormalities are due to those same imperfections, in which our strange traditions about sex education are one element. The number of sex offenders in our prisons is considerable. An acquaintance with the processes of trial in such cases reveals striking differences of attitude on the part of judges and magistrates with, on the whole, a tendency to get away from the reaction of emotional condemnation towards a more understanding state of mind.

CHAPTER VI

MENTAL DEFECT

MENTAL DEFECT

MENTAL defect in its old sense signifies an inborn deficiency of intelligence. Among psychologists there has been much discussion as to what intelligence is and whether there is a general quality of intelligence running through all the mental processes involved in understanding our environment. Perhaps one might describe intelligence as the faculty of perceiving relationships or, one might say, of putting two and two together.

If this faculty is weak or missing then we have a series beginning with the dullard who is just a bit below the average, who finds school lessons difficult and, unless some special aptitude exists and is discovered, must perforce be content with a subordinate position in life, though he is quite able to look after himself and perhaps a family. There is no decided line between him and the high-grade mental defective in whom there is need for some care and consideration to enable him to fit into social life. Next comes the grades of defect that have been legally defined as feeble-mindedness, imbecility, and idiocy, for which care and treatment are arranged by the provisions of the Mental Deficiency Act. It is laid down, for legal purposes, that mental defect must have existed before the age of eighteen years, whether it be inborn or due to disease or injury.

The degree of defect in these cases is usually expressed in terms of "mental age," as compared with the real or "chronological" age. The idiot does not develop beyond the stage normal for a two-year-old, the imbecile beyond that of a three to seven-year-old, whilst the mental age of the feeble-minded may range from seven to twelve years.

Many tests have been devised for the measurement of intelligence, their aim being to measure innate ability independent of educational influence. There are pitfalls in their use in inexperienced hands, but tests are absolutely necessary both to a scientific study of this subject and to a useful understanding of the individual. Whatever principles may have been applied in their formulation, all standard tests have been thoroughly tried out on large numbers of children and their results measured against the results of other methods of observation. If a few thousand supposedly normal children of five can deal successfully with eight out of ten of a set of questions, if those known to be dull can only deal with less than eight, and some brighter than the rest can deal with nine or ten, then we have a reasonably correct measure of what a normal five-year-old should be able to do on that test. Then it remains to be worked out how far that test measures all the capabilities of the individual child; it is desirable, for example, that trials of mechanical aptitude should supplement trials of perception and verbal description. Indeed, though one speaks of the result of an intelligence test, yet that test is often made up of a battery of different tests, and to the expert a patchy result may be significant. Obvious mistakes in testing are to confuse backwardness through external circumstances, such as illness or parental neglect, with innate defect; to miss the significance of emotional difficulties that not only hinder learning but actually interfere with the tests themselves; to regard sensory defect (deaf-mutism, for example) as part of the disease picture that includes the intellectual defect instead of recognizing it as the cause of the apparent defect. We have all heard of Helen Keller who, becoming deaf and blind at the age of nineteen months, under competent instruction acquired the power of speech and showed high intelligence.

It is often useful to measure the intelligence of adults, and here some standard other than mental age is necessary, for intelligence shows no measurable growth once adolescence is reached. It might be useful to say of a thirty-year-old mental defective that he has a mental age of ten, but the normal variability of adult intelligence calls for another standard. For this purpose an "intelligence quotient" is taken at 100 and the majority of us show quotients that fall between 110 and 90, the upper limit being somewhere about 140, which would indicate a very high intelligence indeed, anything higher being the attribute of a genius; whilst 120 would indicate an intelligence the owner of which could be expected to profit by a university education. As the quotient falls from 90 we approach the level of the dullard.

In the devising of adult tests it has been difficult to exclude the influence of education, for obviously verbal or numerical tests cannot avoid that influence, and many quite useful methods must also serve to some extent as tests of education. Very ingenious, however, is Raven's matrix test, which consists of patterns of increasing degrees of complexity, from which a portion is missing. The victim is required to select the missing portion from a variety offered him, and for this task ordinary education gives no help. The writer essayed this test and failed to complete it, thus being compelled to acknowledge its searching quality, though he was comforted by the assurance that his performance would put him in the top fifteen of a sample of a hundred of the general population.

This description of the use of tests must not be taken to indicate that they are the beginning and end of investigation. The whole history of the individual must be studied. To the skilled psychologist his way of tackling the tests, or his behaviour during them, may give as much information as the test itself. Indeed, I would ask the reader to picture the test not so much as a diagnostic procedure as a confirmation of what has already been observed or suspected and a practical way of expressing degrees of defect or capability. (Sometimes it turns out to be a refutation of a false diagnosis of mental defect, for a good performance is positive evidence that cannot be denied.)

SOME CAUSES OF MENTAL DEFECT

There is obviously a wide range of variability within biological limits—that is, a degree of dullness or feeble-mindedness can occur that is not indicative of any diseased state but comes at the lower end of the scale that includes ordinary folk. Intelligence varies just as stature does; but as there are diseases producing physical dwarfism so there are diseases causing a lack of intellectual development. Most of

E*

these only interest the specialist, but some have a general interest.

One of these is cretinism, a condition that can be recognized in early infancy. The child fails to develop physically and mentally, and a characteristic picture of bodily abnormalities appears. At the best the sufferer belongs to the group of feeble-minded, though he is harmless and good-tempered and, indeed, often receives a more than usual share of maternal affection. The disease was long known to be due to an inborn deficiency in secretion of the thyroid gland, occurred in geographical association with other disease of the thyroid gland and was almost certainly related to a lack of iodine in the drinking water, though it may occur in isolated cases where that factor is not likely to be present. Then it was found that complete surgical removal of a diseased thyroid gland was followed by symptoms identical with myxoedema, a disease already known in which the gland had atrophied; next it was discovered that the continued administration of the dried gland obtainable from animals would restore the patient to health. From this it was a natural step to try thyroid extract on sufferers from cretinism, and one of the miracles of medicine happened. If the case was taken early enough the picture changed and natural growth, physical and mental, took place. But the patient must take thyroid extract for the rest of his life, like the adult sufferer from myxoedema.

Another clearly inborn disorder is Mongolism, a puzzling condition in which the infant resembles in facial characteristics the Mongol race, even in that apparent slant of the eyes which is really caused by a fold in the upper eyelid, with changes in the shape of the skull, and other physical abnormalities. Mentally the development takes on the same general pattern as the cretin—idiocy, imbecility or feeble-mindedness, combined with good temper and tractability—but nothing is known about the basis of the trouble except for some evidence that there is occasionally a family element concerned. Nor does any physical treatment help.

Half a dozen other kinds of inborn mental defect arising from physical causes could be enumerated, like the Mongol and the cretin. The influence of alcohol in the parent upon mental defect in the offspring has been strongly asserted and almost as strongly denied, and whilst it is generally believed that defective parents will breed a defective stock, yet the proportion of such parents in the population is subject to very different estimates, and defective children have an unfortunate way of being born to normal parents. Some pedigrees have been published showing dramatic and disastrous results of the hereditary transmission of mental defect, but they are not regarded as quite reliable. That aspect of the subject is now being carefully investigated. Hereditary syphilis certainly plays a part in producing mental defect, but the defect is obviously secondary to the syphilis.

SOCIAL ASPECT OF MENTAL DEFECT

An old-standing social problem is concerned with these cases of mental defect that stand towards the lower end of the scale of biological variability. Those defectives low enough down the scale to be recognized and cared for from childhood onwards are not so much a problem as a responsibility and expense to the community. Segregation in institutions is a humane way of caring for those unfitted to stand up to the needs of ordinary life, and gives an opportunity of training them to be useful and sometimes even to take up outside life in conditions where they can be to some extent protected from greater demands than they are capable of meeting. The treatment of those a little higher in the scale is not so easy to decide. In this connexion a reference to the work of army psychiatrists in the late war will be useful.

So long as the musket was the most complicated weapon in which he needed to be proficient, the high-grade feeble-minded young man probably made a most efficient soldier; indeed, the combination of implicit obedience on the part of the private and paternal solitude on the part of the officer that was a tradition in some of our most famous regiments might have been evolved to suit him. The demands of modern warfare are totally different and soldiers with an intelligence quotient (I.Q.) of 80 or so could not meet them. It had not been possible to eliminate or separate all of these men on enlistment, and such action was even opposed by medical men in high places who had little sympathy with psychological medicine. Combatant officers associated with training soon learned, however, what the psychiatrists had to offer them and were ready to collect all their difficult cases—the man who was always in trouble for petty offences, the one who repeatedly went sick with trivial complaints and especially the stupid ones that couldn't be taught. With regard to the last group—obviously those with a low I.Q.—the curious observation was made that a man's fellow-soldiers would often recognize his inability to look after himself and take upon themselves to care for him and keep him out of trouble, with the result that his condition might for a long time escape recognition.

The adjutant, let us suppose, has now prepared a list of his difficult cases and the psychiatrist is asked to examine them. He finds a mixed bag of psychoneurotics, dullards, round pegs in square holes, and what-not, but it is the fate of the dullards that concerns us just now. If they are otherwise fit they are transferred to a unit with quite a well-sounding name but manned almost entirely by dullards and high-grade feeble-minded soldiers, who are no longer expected to become efficient at technical matters but are given work, often hard physical work, well within their capacity. Looked after by officers and N.C.O.'s who know what they have to deal with, these men now become useful and contented members of the army community.

Outstanding cases of mental defect, whose recognition is obvious, leave very little room for doubt. They must be looked after, and that's that. Where lesser degrees are concerned, and the individual has been expected to take his place in the world like anyone else, trouble may or may not arise. If a lad is emotionally stable and good tempered but with an I.Q., let us suppose, of 80, he may be lucky enough to find work within his scope and acquire a reputation for reliability and good behaviour so long as no demands are made that he cannot meet. Even then he may come to grief. I recall a young man whose fingers were gnarled with years of work in handling raw hides all day and every day, the sort of work that anyone with a normal I.Q. would get out of as soon as possible. Then, being physically normal, when his sex feelings woke up he committed a foolish offence that brought him within the attention of the law. I am glad to say that his good record, and a definite appraisement of his mental capabilities, were considered by the court and steps were taken for some kindly supervision instead of the prison sentence that would have been almost a routine not so long ago.

Failing the luck of a suitable job, our lad is likely to shift from one occupation to another and acquire a bad reputation accordingly. Here the slightly subnormal often fares the worse, for he may become vexed and dissatisfied by his failure and seek to remedy it by illegitimate efforts in the direction of criminal offences. It is now well recognized that there is an excess of mental defectives among delinquents—or, at least, among those who are found out—and that the delinquency may originate in the defective himself or may result from the influence of others.

Another occasional manifestation crops up in cases of child neglect, when a mentally defective parent proves incapable of shouldering the responsibility of a family.

EMOTIONAL OR MORAL DEFECT

Here we are faced by difficulties of definition. As noted above, mental defect may lead to criminal or other anti-social behaviour, but the mental defect can be diagnosed quite independently of that behaviour. There are, however, cases in which there is persistent misconduct—lying, stealing, cruelty and the like—not controlled by punishment nor bringing obvious profit or advantage to the mis-doer, in which no intellectual defect can be recognized. At one time there was given to this sort of offender the title of "moral imbecile," now changed to "moral defective." But morality is not inborn, it is a result of training and example; the normal child accepts the moral code of his surroundings, and fortunately those surroundings are generally representative of our social code; if brought up in criminal surroundings, the potentially normal child will accept the code of that little world. There must be some mental factor that by its presence or absence interferes with the acceptance of the social code in the cases of persistent inability to recognize its importance.

Let us first eliminate cases in which there can be detected a cause for the misconduct, misconduct which turns out to bear some relation to "nervous" symptoms arising from unconscious mental processes. An actual example will help us to understand.

A bright little fellow of seven years would repeatedly expose his penis to small girls, expostulation and punishment having no effect upon his behaviour. To the examining psychologist he declared, "I don't want to do it," and this statement, put forth reasonably and intelligently, was enough to place the action in the category of "compulsive behaviour" and raise hopes of dealing with it successfully. After two or three interviews, at which he set himself to explore the honesty and reliability of his physician by a stream of questions, he suddenly blurted out, "What's a little girl like?" and, his questions being given straightforward answers, he pursued the subject till he extracted an account of the process of childbirth. He was told nothing that he did not ask about, though he was shown a photograph of the Neapolitan Venus and rather admired it, and when he had obviously satisfied his curiosity he expressed that fact by announcing, "I don't want to come here any more." The matter of exposing himself had never been mentioned after the first interview, but now he was asked about it and replied, "I shan't do that again: not ever." To Macaulay's Londoner, who so rarely makes a mistake in the use of *shall* and *will*, it will be plain that this very intelligent chap was not making a promise but stating a fact. He knew he was cured. We may, if we like, try to imagine how his impulse of curiosity—repressed by an old-fashioned and prudish nanny—came to expression in the reverse impulse. The episode suggests an origin of those examples in which an adult gets into trouble for indecent exposure, and suggests, too, that punishment may not entirely satisfy the needs of the occasion.

Healy, of the Children's Court at Chicago, gave many examples in his book *Mental Conflict and Misconduct*, published some twenty-five years ago, of stealing, truancy, and such-like, in which unsolved problems, generally connected with sex matters, were operative.

Sometimes the lack of parental affection, or a fancied belief in the lack, may produce similar reactions; there is, indeed, no limit to the strange hidden urges capable of producing these disorders of conduct.

In a case I was familiar with, a lad realized, as a result of treatment, that his mixed feelings of love and hatred towards his parents often put him in a dilemna when they desired some action to be taken by him. When that happened, an impulse to steal arose (it seemed to indicate the idea that as he could not get affection he would take something else), and yielding to it gave him a strange relief of tension. He benefited by this realization, though the ambivalent feeling to the parents persisted. Later on, when discussing plans for his future and his father's proposals about them, he pointed out how in one respect the plans might go wrong; "Then," said he, "if I couldn't tell Dad, I might start pinching again."

In such cases as these where, after psychological investigation, specific causes are found to be concerned in the production of the misconduct, there is no need to postulate an inherent defect. Eliminating those, and also those in which intellectual defect is demonstrable, we are left with a group of people, young and old, who are persistently abnormal in their behaviour and seem to have no guiding principles that will enable them to appreciate the significance of their own lack of conformity with the demands of society.

TEMPERAMENTAL DEFECTIVES

Sir Cyril Burt has proposed the above name to indicate this class of difficult person, and the term implies some emotional defect. I find this a useful conception, and, to indicate how emotion enters into the question, must make a few dogmatic but reasonably orthodox assertions.

Man possesses instincts that serve as driving forces to behaviour, reason being rather a tool than a driving force. (If the reader feels that I am committing the crime of "dethroning reason" I invite him to read his daily paper.) These instincts may be described and classified according to taste, and they bear with them an emotion that gives them feeling value to the individual. The parental instinct, for example, bears the emotion of tenderness and if this emotion is lacking the parent may carry out his duty to his offspring but at times behave with an entire lack of tenderness that will appear unaccountable to the more ordinary onlooker. Man is a social animal, the member of a herd, and we must postulate an instinct that holds the herd together. It is not easy to define the associated emotion, but it is convenient to think of it as having a positive and a negative side; on the positive side we have sympathy—some psychologists put suggestibility here—for the members of the herd tend to experience the same emotions and hold the same beliefs; and on the negative side the emotion of shame when disapproval of the herd is perceived. In the temperamental defectives both these emotions are lacking. To be in emotional harmony with their fellows is beyond their experience, and to feel shame is impossible. The intellectual perception of the moral code then carries no drive with it, and the satisfaction of material desires becomes the only urge, without that appreciation of the emotional reactions of his fellows which produces a normal feeling of shame.

An extreme example of this condition has recently been before the public eye. A man committed two murders to the accompaniment of sadistic actions with means that were described with horrible detail in the press.[1] His history showed years of anti-social offences, sometimes necessitating considerable ability and intelligence, and bringing with them punishments and penalties; they were offences that could have brought only temporary satisfaction. After the murders he showed little idea of planning to escape detection and even made callous and unnecessary reference to the crime before his actual detection. At the trial he showed unconcern. After condemna-

[1] To the psychologist there are cogent reasons why such reports should not be published. The publicity given to the efforts of young women to gain admission to the trial indicated the emotions that were stimulated. To put it bluntly, whilst accounts of normal sex behaviour are excluded on moral grounds, lurid accounts of abnormal sex behaviour, with descriptions of the means used, are given free play to stimulate abnormal tendencies. I suppose everyone would approve of a press censorship if he could be the censor, and this is where I should like to exercise authority.

tion the question of his insanity was enquired into by experts appointed by the Home Office, but the capital sentence was carried out. I can experience neither intellectual nor emotional interest as to whether he should have been judged insane, but I think the society that is content to treat the habitual offender with repeated punishment and let it go at that is asking for trouble.

Cases such as the above abound in literature, and there is such a similarity in them that we must suppose there is a cause common to them all. The explanation given above is hypothetical and is not capable of proof as in the case of the seven-year-old boy, where we find a sequence of cause and effect in the treatment which any reasonable person can accept. Unfortunately, the temperamental defective could not co-operate in any attempt to unravel the cause of his trouble, so it is impossible to establish conclusively that the condition is inborn and not the result of early influences after birth. To picture it as due to the emotional defect described above is the likeliest and easiest hypothesis; but that hypothesis may be wrong.

Fortunately, such serious forms of the trouble are comparatively rare. More often there is a continued series of stupid escapades and scrapes, failures to hold a job, and shady transactions with ever-increasing risk of conflict with the law. Behind an apparent affection for the parents there is continued disregard of their feelings and of the difficulties in which they are placed by the behaviour of the offender. He may be well up to the average intelligence and ready enough to admit the unreasonableness of his behaviour, but this admission carries with it no emotional conviction.

Although I have drawn a distinction between the accidentally occurring disorder of behaviour and the inborn type, and this distinction is often of great importance, yet the desire to put cases into pigeon-holes must not become an end in itself. A common mistake is that of being satisfied with superficial explanations of pathological behaviour. A beautiful example occurred some years ago when a lad informed the police that he had pushed someone into a canal and drowned him. The canal was dragged, but no body was found, nor could anyone be found missing in the neighbourhood, so the lad was brought to court and charged with an offence the specification of which I forget. There he received a stern admonition, being told that he had done this just to draw attention to himself and mustn't do it again. A psychiatric colleague wrote to a medical journal pointing out the danger of this casual treatment of what might be a serious condition, and soon afterwards was able to write again and give justification for his warning. The lad had now set fire to a ship and the need for examination of his mental condition had become manifest. He was probably a schizophrenic.

I must here pay tribute to the changes that are taking place in this regard. The psychologist is no longer viewed by the public and some lawyers as having as his only aim that of saving the offender from punishment. Provision is being made for psychological help in our courts and the *Institute for the Scientific Treatment of Delinquency* receives useful support in the efforts indicated by its title. Yet it is twenty years since Dr. Hamblin Smith in his *Psychology of the Criminal* laid down the essentials of the subject as worked out in his prison experience.

This case leads on to the subject of pathological lying. The lies are generally phantasies, the telling of which appears to satisfy something lacking in the patient's life; perhaps they deal with wealth and position, perhaps they are romances of performance and triumph on the part of the teller. He does not believe them himself—or they would be delusions—and it has sometimes appeared to me that the satisfaction derived from them depends upon the feeling that, in telling them, he has somehow scored a triumph over the listener. Sometimes, joined with pathological stealing, pathological lying seems again to be a type reaction standing in a group by itself. These people are cheerful and, of course, communicative; they show a relation to the emotionally defectives described above. When the condition is fully developed, a form of behaviour follows with which newspaper readers are familiar. The offender acts as if his phantasies were true, stays at an expensive hotel, in war-time wears uniform and puts up decorations of no mean order, and for a time carries off his deceit in a way that should rouse the envy of the professional swindler. Again it seems as if his satisfaction must be derived from his triumph over other people rather than from his material gains.[1]

KLEPTOMANIA

Everyone knows about this form of pathological stealing, and some of us know the story of the magistrate who announced, in reply to the plea of kleptomania, "Yes: that's the disease I am here to cure," though few know what the victim thought but didn't say, "Yes, that's all right, but how are you going to do it?"

It differs from other forms of pathological stealing in being confined to stealing and stealing only. Fortunately, many kleptomaniacs have insight into their condition and are willing, even anxious, to co-operate in psychological investigation; it is not unknown for them to seek treatment before falling into the hands of the law.

Sometimes the thefts are confined to articles of a particular kind, which may be stored up and not put to any material use or advantage. In such cases the nature or shape of the stolen articles may turn out to have a symbolic meaning for the victim. Healy showed—and this has been confirmed by others—that the offence might result from sexual urges unrecognized by the patient uutil revealed in the course of treatment. In some of his cases the sexual urge was not towards action but towards thoughts that had been suppressed because of their repugnant nature or the social prohibition placed upon them. The urge to commit one offence then found an outlet in committing another less repugnant. Some writers have given the victim's account of a state of mental and physical stress, produced by resisting the impulse to steal and removed by yielding to it.

These considerations should satisfy us that kleptomania does exist as a definite pathological impulse apart from any

[1] These and other varieties of behaviour-disorder stopping short of insanity and without intellectual defect yet often associated with alcoholism, drug addiction, quarrelsomeness and what-not, are, as a matter of convenience, brought together under the heading of "psychopathic personality." It is a useful phrase when it becomes necessary to put a name to a case, but it must not be taken to indicate any knowledge of cause or, indeed, any accuracy of definition.

acquisitive gain. Nobody knows how many of the cases of shoplifting that come to the courts are of this nature, but I have my own view as to one possible factor. Patients with a pathological tendency occasionally describe the stimulating effect of newspaper reports of actions like those to which they have the tendency. This especially applies to behaviour associated with sex perversion, such as damaging women's clothes or cutting hair, occasional epidemics of which sometimes occur, but any pathological urge can be thus stimulated and I suggest that the more reports of shoplifting are put in the papers the more shoplifting there will be.

If the above view as to the nature of kleptomania is correct, then it should not have been discussed here but in the section dealing with the psychoneuroses. It seemed advisable, however, to consider it in conjunction with other cases of pathological stealing and to let it serve as an example of the wide psychological difference that can underlie a superficial resemblance of symptoms.

We are faced, then, with two groups of pathological delinquents. In one group the delinquency arises from unconscious urges that depend upon a more or less accidental set of circumstances and are capable of elucidation by some kind of analytical procedure, the elucidation having often a curative effect. In the other group the urges may be those common to most of us but restrained in us by our emotional acceptance of the moral code; the delinquent is, perhaps by inborn defect, incapable of this emotional recognition and is not restrained by the intellectual recognition of their wrongfulness, nor is he permanently deterred by punishment or the threat of punishment. He becomes a victim to passing moods and desires, readily expresses penitence, and tends to repeat his offences in spite of it. He may sometimes be helped by talks with an understanding person and by putting him, as far as possible, in a position in which he can satisfy his reasonable needs without being tempted to satisfy them by anti-social acts. By such means an adjustment to life has sometimes been reached.

This separation into two groups must take into account that the temperamental defective is not, as such, immune from pathological urges different from the normal instincts; his stealing may show the selective characters of that of the other group and, if he is co-operative, its cause may be similarly elucidated. Or he may react to his difficulties with psycho-neurotic symptoms. Once again, diagnosis must depend upon careful study of the individual case.

The legal position is often very difficult. Whatever the patient's social position, he or she may be a cause of expense and worry to the family, with constant fear of publicity. Yet the behaviour is not as a rule such as to make it possible to certify insanity, and only if the condition has been present from a very early age can the patient be brought within the scope of the Mental Deficiency Act, and treated as a "moral defective."

Doctors and lawyers have often been unable to agree on these cases since the law so far can only recognize the alterna-tives of sanity and insanity, and the legal definition of insanity takes account only of the intellectual criterion. Yet it is becom-ing more and more recognized that there are people whose knowledge, education and intelligence are within normal limits, but whose behaviour is so grossly and persistently anti-social that they are in frequent conflict with the law and are never-theless not influenced by punishment or emotional recognition of the nature of their misdeeds; moreover, as the capital crime described above makes quite clear, there is the ever-present risk of their committing the most terrible misdeeds. Possibly the solution may be non-punitive segregation under an inde-terminate sentence, so that both investigation and treatment might go hand in hand and the public would be protected.

The appearance in this chapter of an example of sadistic murder as a manifestation of temperamental defect shows the overlapping that occurs when, for descriptive purposes, we try to group our cases. A sex perversion can occur as an isolated symptom in a man who is in other respects a happy and normally adjusted member of society. I have seen clear-cut homo-sexuality in such a person. It may be associated with obsessional or anxiety symptoms which psychoanalysis may show to be related to it in origin. Its most important combination, however, is with temperamental defect and one well-known authority has recently pointed out that the delinquent psychopath (a temperamental defective) is frequently also a sexual pervert.

It is only a matter of opinion, but the authority I refer to would probably agree that this apparent frequency may be deceptive. There are many more examples of perversion, sometimes of mild degree, among ordinary people than is generally thought, and they may not be incompatible with a normal sex life; indeed, the person concerned may have only a dim awareness of the presence of a perversion and no awareness of its significance, the tendency being to thrust it aside as a strange and undesirable personal peculiarity, the overt expression of which cannot be tolerated by the instinct of the herd or the super-ego.

In the psychopath, however, these controlling forces are inoperative. Hence what in the ordinary man would remain as a vague and hardly recognized tendency is now allowed to reach the surface and obtain gratification without any consideration of results.

The psychological treatment of psychopathic delinquents, including sexual offenders of that group, has hitherto been regarded as offering greater difficulties than the treatment of the psychoneurotic offender. In a recent communication, however, Dr. Glover, the chairman of the Scientific Committee of the Institute referred to on a previous page, says that this assumption proves to be ill-founded and that the psychopath clearly proves his amenability to "manipulation" of his psychic situation.

CHAPTER VII

PSYCHOSES

PSYCHOSES

IN our second chapter it was explained that the popular distinction between *nervous* and *mental* was misleading and the alternative classification of *psychoneurosis* and *psychosis* was better. The classification into sane and insane is a legal matter, not medical; to head this chapter "insanities," though it might appear to be using simple language, would interfere with understanding. A man suffering from melancholia can, in some circumstances, be cared for at home without great risk or trouble and without any need for restraint; he is legally sane, for his symptoms may be so mild that it is impossible, as well as unnecessary, to certify him as insane. Another man with the same disease of mind, melancholia, may be so uncontrolled and uncontrollable that for his own safety he must be placed somewhere where he can be properly nursed and protected from harm. But if he cannot or will not consent to this procedure, no one has any right to compel him unless certain legal formalities devised for his protection are carried out. This is "certification" and he is then described as being insane or of unsound mind. Yet his disease is the same as that of the other man who is being cared for at home, so to set up a classification into *sane* and *insane*, and to head this chapter "insanity," would be a spurious simplification.

MIND AND BRAIN

Without going into metaphysical questions about the relationship of brain and mind, some principles can be laid down.

(a) *Disease of brain can exist without disease of mind.* An apoplectic stroke is generally caused by haemorrhage into the brain, when the patient may lose the use of arm and leg on one side and become unable to articulate intelligibly. His mind remains clear, though sometimes deterioration may take place, with, perhaps, some interference with memory or growth of irritability.

Speech, writing, the understanding of the written or printed word, the ability to name things or people, the recognition of the use of everyday articles like a pencil or key, and many other specific activities may be interfered with by disease, and these disturbances have given us much information about the localization of such functions in the different parts of the brain. Although speech and writing and such-like acts are mental as well as physical, yet in these troubles it is generally agreed that the mind as a whole, or the personality of the patient, is unaffected. The mind is still healthy but its tool, the brain, is damaged.

Tumours of the brain sometimes produce physical signs and symptoms only; they cause increased pressure within the skull and this may result in loss of comprehension, apathy, and irritability. A definite psychosis caused by a brain tumour is rare.

(b) *Disease of mind, or psychosis, can exist without known disease of brain.* Most of the patients in our mental hospitals are examples of such disease.

(c) *Not only disease of brain, but disease of body, infections, toxins, and disturbances of nutrition, can produce psychoses.*

Category (a) does not concern us here. The next category, however, comprising the majority of mental hospital patients, is of the highest importance. It is convenient to put these patients into diagnostic groups, and as a general rule if our grouping, or diagnosis, is correct it enables us to plan treatment and to some extent foretell the progress of the case. Whether our groups represent separate disease entities may be left undecided till we know more about their causes; there is often an overlapping, and the patient has to be under observation for a shorter or longer period before the diagnosis can be regarded as certain.

PSYCHOSES MARKED BY DISORDERED MOOD-REACTIONS
(Affective Disorders)

These psychoses are essentially pathological exaggerations of the normal moods of sadness or elation. The sadness becomes melancholia, elation becomes mania, and both are out of relation with reality. Kretschmer has made studies of the physique of such people and claims that they are marked by the predominance of a build he calls "pyknic"; short, thick-set folk—the type that Australian idiom picturesquely describes as "nuggety." In contrast are those of the long-limbed, muscular, athletic type, which he regards as more frequently seen among the sufferers from schizophrenia (split mind). Other observers believe that there are mental characteristics marking those who later become manic or melancholic; they are either cheery, talkative people, sometimes aggressive, or they take a gloomy outlook upon life and magnify its troubles.

As to the cause of these disorders we are handicapped by the fact that it is impossible to apply psychoanalytical methods to the patient when he is either manic or melancholic; the only opportunity for such procedure comes during the intermissions that occur in the disease, and the actual findings in such cases do not carry with them the clearness and certainty that is obtained in the analysis of the psychoneuroses. There is plenty of interesting deduction from observation, especially by the practitioners of child analysis, but I cannot feel that anything like certainty has been obtained by that method of approach, though it seems very promising. The principle that emerges is that they are due to deep-seated disturbances in the development of the emotions and instincts, disturbances which lie in the unconscious till they become manifest as the psychosis.

Of course the natural tendency is to look to external stress for causes of depression, and psychiatrists are in agreement that sometimes it is responsible. Such cases they call "reactive depression." Usually, however, the trouble comes out of the blue, though the first indication of it may be worrying about something trivial. Relatives may think this initial worrying is a "cause" but it is not; it is a danger signal.

It was only in 1896 that Kraepelin brought under the heading of *manic-depressive psychosis* various disorders that had appeared to be unrelated and gave us a useful conception that has helped our understanding of them.

He showed that mania and melancholia are phases of the same disorder. There may be a cycle in which melancholia, mania and normality form a continuous procession, the patient passing from one to the other in a repeated sequence; or one phase, generally the manic, does not occur, so that the sequence is melancholia, normality, melancholia.

MELANCHOLIA

In its simplest form we see recurrent periods of a mild depression that may not interfere seriously with the patient's activities. Although mild, they should not be regarded lightly, and it is one of the difficulties of the condition that the patient's friends and relatives, seeing no signs of physical illness, may not recognize its true nature. It is characteristic of these depressions, of any degree, that the patient blames himself. In the mildest form he may say he "ought to have pulled himself together sooner and not got like this." Or he may blame his illness upon some real or imagined misdeed, and, as the grade of severity increases, he complains of unworthiness and may develop delusions of having committed some unpardonable sin. It is to be noted that such delusions are not primary manifestations of the illness but arise because of the depression.

It is probable that there is no break between those changes of mood that are common to many of us, and the mildest forms of melancholia. These are often called cyclothymia, and are marked by recurrent bouts of depression, loss of mental and physical energy, and perhaps some awareness of loss of the capacity of feeling affection. Sometimes the periodicity is so notable that it can be marked on a calendar and shown to follow a regular time-table; in duration the attacks may vary from a few days to weeks or months, the patient being able, in the milder cases, to carry on with his work, though with difficulty. In the more severe cases the appearance may change, the man becoming careworn and old-looking. He declares that he is a disgrace and a failure, blames himself for it all and wishes he were dead. His thoughts are obviously slow and he delays in answering questions. Action, too, is retarded and he may, if left alone, sit and mope all day. Yet he knows all that is happening, where he is, and may recognize that he is ill and express his willingness to enter a mental hospital. This last characteristic, is, happily, often present in a patient who has had previous attacks, and when an attack is impending he may sometimes spontaneously arrange for his own admission.

Physical symptoms are often complained of, vague and mostly concerned with the digestive organs.

Recovery from the attack takes place as a rule, whatever treatment is adopted, though cases occur that may last for years or never recover. The following personal experience is instructive:

"When I was in practice in Shanghai a well-to-do Chinese gentleman fell sick with various physical complaints not falling into any diagnostic combination I was familiar with. He was full of woe, declared himself unable to carry on with his ordinary affairs, and sat at home with his troubles. I diagnosed his condition as neurasthenia and attended to teeth, stomach, and everything else I could find to treat. At last he tired of my efforts and turned to a continental colleague who injected him with what was then, I believe, a favourite remedy in his own country—sea-water carefully sterilized and diluted down to the same saline concentration as the blood. After a few of these injections the patient was cured and I began to think there might after all be some virtue in isotonic sea-water.

"After a year or so the illness returned. This time the sea-water failed to work a cure, the illness dragged on for months, and the patient, who still remained my very good friend, was in the depths of despair. Then he suddenly recovered at time when no treatment was being given, and I was more puzzled than ever.

"Looking back upon the case it becomes clear as a recurrent melancholia, and it illustrates the fact that, in this self-limited disorder, the treatment the patient is receiving when he recovers gets the credit for curing him."

In the severer forms of depression the bodily symptoms and gloomy outlook take on a delusional form, though memory and the intellectual powers may otherwise remain unaffected.

The handling of the patient's relatives is sometimes the initial difficulty in treatment. They tend to urge him to effort, unless in time they come to recognize that such urging is futile. They may have an aversion to treatment in a mental hospital, especially when the patient's mind is still clear, and one can hardly tell them bluntly that in a mental illness relatives generally do more harm than good.

It is an old rule that every melancholic is a potential suicide, and it is only too common to read of that tragedy when the details show to the informed reader that the diagnosis of melancholia had been missed or not acted upon.

MANIA

Mania is marked by an unstable mood of elation, a rapid flow of ideas, and a combination of excessive mental and physical activity. Here again there are infinite gradations from a state hardly more cheerful than what is regarded as healthy, to a state where disordered conversation and conduct make institutional treatment imperative, where, indeed, the patient conforms to the old idea of a "raving lunatic." In some cases alternating with mild cyclothymic attacks the relatives may accept the elated phase as a "turn for the good" and be disappointed when it is followed by a return to what is the patient's normal self. On an earlier page it was noted that some observers describe cheery, talkative people, sometimes aggressive, as one type that becomes melancholic or manic. If we exaggerate those qualities a little we have that condition called chronic hypomania, which may last for years before swinging over to its opposite.

The mildly elated may present a problem of control, for there is never an insight into the illness as in the case of the melancholic. I have known of relatives being sadly bothered about a mildly manic person who insists upon driving a car, and I suspect that some people who get into trouble for driving offences are hypomaniacs, though for obvious reasons that condition is not likely to be raised as a plea in defence.

This account of a most important group is highly simplified. There is nothing to be gained by enumerating the many varieties and combinations of these conditions, or the distressing symptoms that occur. One may mention, however, that form called involutional melancholia, which affects persons of both sexes at a time when some of the bodily functions are declining. It differs in several respects from the typical form and recovery tends to be prolonged.

After childbirth a psychosis may develop, and it may be one of several types, but melancholia is the commonest. Those cases of infanticide in which the mother is found to be insane are generally melancholias. Recovery is the rule and the patient may be expected to return to her ordinary life.

SCHIZOPHRENIA OR SPLIT MIND

In 1896 Kraepelin, besides classifying the manic-depressive group, separated another to which he gave the name of dementia praecox. The name signified that the condition occurred early and finally showed a permanent dementia. Experience taught that these elements were not invariable and in 1911 the term schizophrenia was introduced to indicate much the same group of cases but with less narrow limitations. It covers a steady deterioration of the personality, usually starting in adolescence, and involving disorder of feeling, conduct and thought.

Many ph ical changes have been found in the disease but there is no agreement as to any being the cause of it. In prolonged cases there certainly occur profound changes in bodily well-being, together with alterations of nerve cells which themselves may be a reaction to various bodily conditions.

Heredity seems to play a part in determining its incidence, and in most cases where a complete history is worked out there emerge indications early in life of premonitory vagaries of behaviour. Often the child is intellectually above the average but seclusive, forming few friends, and given to day-dreaming. To this kind of temperament is sometimes given the name of schizoid, and it stands in contrast to the manic-depressive temperament described on a previous page. One well-known authority, Adolf Meyer, concluded that schizophrenia was the end result of an accumulation of faulty habits of reaction.

This accords with the fact that the disorder is of slow development. The symptoms are extraordinarily varied and the behaviour disorders may range from mild eccentricity to troublesome or dangerous activities. The patient seems to be living in a strange world of phantasy with its own distorted logic and conceptions, as shown by bizarre emotional reactions and delusions. Contact with reality may be entirely lost so that he may sit like a mummy, with vacant face and no show of interest in the outside world, entirely wrapped up in his phantasy life. It is this conception of his living in a world of his own, with only a part or none of his personality now concerned with real life, that has given us the idea of the split mind.

Some observers have noted that if the apparently senseless chatter of a schizophrenic is studied, or if his delusions are investigated, their mental content proves to be the same as that which is found in the laborious psychoanalysis of a psychoneurotic or even of a "normal" person. In the last two cases its fantastic or unreal relation to ordinary life is recognized as soon as the material is brought to consciousness; in the case of the schizophrenic he is actually living in, and elaborating, that world of the unconscious, and the real world has become the unreal. It seems that this gives a useful idea of what he is doing. Why he does it is a question the answer to which may give us the key to the disease.

The outlook is not so bad as was once believed, when it was said that if a case of dementia praecox recovered, then the diagnosis had been wrong; that belief no longer prevails as regards schizophrenia. A great deal can be done by care and attention to keep the victim in touch with reality and help him to lead some sort of social life. Early diagnosis should be aimed at and adolescent eccentricity should be properly evaluated by the psychiatrist. The failure of reproof or punishment to modify faulty behaviour may be the first sign; and a lasting difficulty in deciding upon a career has more than once caused parents to seek the advice of a vocational psychologist who has been well enough trained to suspect the presence of an early schizophrenia and urge the seeking of proper psychiatric aid.

PARANOIAC REACTIONS

The schizophrenic often shows alterations of mood that link his disorder with the manic-depressive group; but his delusions are not, as it were, deductions from his state of misery. They have their own fantastic logic, as in the youth whose first serious escapade was to claim the right to travel anywhere by train without a ticket, and only after much pressing was he led to explain that, as he was the representative of the Almighty on earth, of course he had that right. Later developments confirmed the diagnosis of split mind, but the symptom might have proved to place him in the next group, paranoia. Schizophrenia, then, has affinities on the one side with the affective disorders, and on the other with paranoia. This, which used to be called delusional insanity, may be regarded as a disorder of the intellect, the emotional effects being secondary. There exists in the paranoiac a group of false ideas, in a typical case of being wronged or persecuted, that cannot be influenced by reason and yet leave the rest of his mind unaffected, (*para*, beside: *noein*, to think: the false ideas being pictured as existing alongside the normal mind.) When the delusional system is not concerned the behaviour of the man is perfectly ordinary; he can go about his business or pleasure without his condition being suspected, though in a fully developed state his persecution beliefs, which may be transformed into grandiose delusions, may lead to anti-social or dangerous behaviour. From one point of view the world is full of mildly paranoiac people: the man with a bee in his bonnet, who converses like other folk till his particular bee is started and then becomes a changed person, irrational and obstinate, so that his friends learn to keep away from the particular topic that starts him off: the man with a grievance, who can think only ill of those he thinks have wronged him and is impervious to hints that he may be misjudging them. These people, however, are mistaken but scarcely deluded. If a man thinks remarks are being made accusing him of, let us say, some sexual offence, he is setting off along another road: if he acts upon that false belief and assaults someone or, being more litigious than pugnacious, makes complaint to the police, he stands a chance of becoming legally insane. From that point he may go on to develop fantastic persecutory ideas that would occupy a page or two of a textbook, ideas that he is being visited at nights by enemies who subject him to all kinds of horrible assaults, that the nurses are being paid to read his thoughts and reveal them to his persecutors, and so on.

It is obvious that such patients will resent their detention in hospital, and it is not surprising that sometimes they try to hide their symptoms and may even succeed to some extent. I recall being present at an interview when a skilled psychiatrist examined such a patient. The man had come into hospital with the history of having assaulted harmless people with no provocation whatever; after a period of good behaviour he was allowed out of the hospital grounds, but had to be brought back at once because he insisted upon walking along the middle of the road among the motor traffic. That was the only evidence of insanity, and for particular reasons it had become necessary to confirm or confute the diagnosis. For nearly an hour I listened while my colleague chatted with the patient, who was quite aware of the reason for the interview. When I was growing thoroughly tired the patient began to tell of people in a particular restaurant who had treated him with disrespect, being apparently unaware of who he was; then he explained that he was of royal blood, and that he had had to chastise some people who would not recognize that fact. Finally he declared that he had the right of way on any public road and that motor cars must give way to him. Until the revealing statement about his royal blood his conversation had been that of a well educated man of the world. It was only the patience and skill of my colleague that elicited the truth as to the delusion.

This was an example of grandiose instead of the more usual persecutory delusion.

The outlook in a fully developed paranoia is very bad, recovery being rare. There are, however, cases that run an episodal course and do not become established. Whether these are really paranoia is a matter for discussion.

As to cause, much has been written. There are some personality types—sensitive and suspicious—that may be predisposed to the disease. A sense of inferiority or repressed desires can be sought as a cause. Sometimes an actual shameful incident associated with guilt may be followed by the feeling that others are aware of it and accusations are based upon that. Freud regarded unconscious homosexuality as the basis of paranoia, but the impossibility of paranoiacs co-operating in psychoanalysis leaves his theory in the air.

In all these psychoses with no known physical cause two views are possible. Firstly, that they are psychologically determined, and if that is the case the search for an organic cause will be futile; secondly, that there exists a hitherto undiscovered bodily cause that may some day be revealed. The discussion of these alternatives rouses remarkable feeling, which depends upon the two different fundamental outlooks described in Chapter I, outlooks that I describe as the psychological and the mechanistic.

TREATMENT

Trained care and supervision, the provision of amenities and of suitable occupation, including occupational therapy under skilled supervision, are, or should be, commonplaces, and of late years new departures have been made in physical treatment of the psychoses dealt with in this chapter.

It was noted that some physical happening, such as an accident or sharp illness, had a beneficial effect upon schizophrenia; as it was known that the injection of an excess of insulin, the drug used to control diabetes, could, by causing a sudden loss of sugar in the blood, produce a state of coma associated with convulsive seizures, such injection was tried out upon schizophrenics. It proved to be harmless and not productive of discomfort, the coma being easily arrested, when judged necessary, by the administration of sugar. Good results were claimed for it and a few years ago the method was popularized in the lay press, with the rather unfortunate result that the relatives of the patients clamoured for its use in unsuitable cases. It has not fulfilled all that was expected of it, but it undoubtedly does good in bringing about a modification of the illness and enabling some patients to be discharged who would otherwise have remained in hospital.

Pursuing the same idea, experimenters found that by using an electric current of suitable strength and nature, applied to the head, it was possible to produce sudden unconsciousness associated with convulsions, which proved to cut short considerably the duration of attacks of melancholia. This electric

F

shock therapy is being tried in other disorders, but the advantage of its use in them is not so well established as in melancholia.

These methods are empirical. That is, they work, but we have no idea how or why they work. A third method has been developed from our knowledge of the localization of brain function, and perhaps I can make clear in a few words how and why that works.

At the base of the brain lie large ganglia, or masses of nerve cells, which, to put it very roughly, serve as collectors of emotion, whether that emotion results from external stimuli or from internal causes such as distressing thoughts. In the fore part of the brain are centres which make that emotion conscious, and they are connected by nerve fibres with the ganglia at the base. An operation, called leucotomy, was designed that severed these fibres and thus cut off emotion from that part of the brain that perceived and felt it. It worked, and, though it must not be advised lightly, it has enabled unruly and noisy schizophrenics to become quiet and even useful members of an institutional society. Melancholics of long standing benefit by it. As one patient put it, "I still have the thoughts but they don't worry me." It has even been used for obsessional cases when the emotional content of the obsession has made life miserable.

The operation in proper hands is fairly safe and the patient experiences but little discomfort. But temperamental changes follow it that are not always advantageous; the bright and intelligent man may become dull and ordinary, the energetic obsessional may become careless and happy-go-lucky. The late effects of such a drastic operation still await observation.

A Discussion of the Make-up of Adolf Hitler

Several attempts have been made to bring the behaviour of Hitler within some diagnostic grouping. The common attribution to him of hysterical displays conveyed little more than a contemptuous judgement, though the history of war-time blindness after gassing may reasonably suggest an hysterical episode. With the help of what the reader has just learnt about the psychoses, it is, I think, possible to present his behaviour as resting upon a manic-depressive personality with paranoiac trends.

He showed remarkable energy and aggressiveness, certainty of belief, ability to plan grandiose schemes, a successful urge to domineer. He could harangue the multitude for hours, and was repetitive and emotional. These are characteristics of a chronic hypomania.

He obviously believed in the truth of his own charges against the Jews of seeking world domination, in his ideas of racial purity, with the Germans as the *élite* of the Aryan race —the conception of an Aryan race being itself irrational. It seems likely that his military adventures were planned more in accord with a belief in German invincibility and his own intuition than in consonance with expert advice. This last may have been a manic quality, but the first two exemplify the growth of a logic-tight system of a paranoid kind.

All went well till the Germans began to be pushed back by the Russians. Then, at a time when his encouraging voice should have been heard, it was silent for months, his subjects being told the unlikely story that he was with his soldiers on the Eastern front. At last it was announced that he would broadcast on a certain date. The speech was postponed for some unconvincing cause and another date was given. A second postponement followed and at last the great leader was heard. But what a change! The loud and compelling voice had gone, and in its place was a flat and toneless reproduction of what was obviously a speech prepared beforehand.

It seems likely that the shock of the reverses in Russia had, as often happens when the manic subject meets a reverse, precipitated a swing-over from the manic to the melancholic. This accounts for the months of silence, and when recovery seemed complete the broadcast was announced; but he was not yet fit for the task and another date was set; when that arrived he again disappointed his medical or political advisers. Only at the third attempt could he face the task and then instead of the aggressive voice of the hypomanic we heard the toneless accents of melancholia. After this the old Hitler was no more;

F*

the hypomanic became just an ordinary human being buffeted by fate, till at last his end was decided by those around him.

Epilepsy

There are several kinds of convulsive seizure to which the name of epilepsy has been given, but it is now generally understood that, when one speaks of epilepsy, a particular kind known as "idiopathic" is meant. In this form stimuli of varied kinds may produce an attack, or attacks may occur without recognizable stimulus; the fundamental cause is still unknown. The nature of the individual attack, what are the physical, chemical or psychological processes that determine it, remains a problem. There is a hereditary element present but, as in all the psychoses, it is not easy to evaluate.

There is described a deterioration of character following the fits, but a modern view is that there are traits of the "epileptic character" existing before the onset of the fits, and the outward manifestations of the disorder result from an original epileptic make-up. The supposed make-up shows a self-satisfied yet sensitive reaction, with protestations of interest, in principles and people, that lack emotional depth. With the progress of the fits the patient loses interest in the world, becomes less and less adjusted to it and finally has to be put under institutional care. This may not happen, however, and many epileptics carry on with their working life.

The convulsions are often replaced by episodal incidents of most varied kind. The man may wander off in a fugue, an epileptic fugue being distinguished from the fugues described in Chapter IV by the apparent impossibility of accounting for it as a dissociation of consciousness with elements of motive. The fugue may cover anything from a few trivial actions to the grossest violations of public order, and the question of epilepsy often arises in our courts.

The fit is often preceded by what is called the epileptic aura—hallucinations of smell or vision, bodily sensations, actual muscular movements and so forth—which may give the patient sufficient warning to protect himself from harm.

There is no need to follow up the ramifications of this

complicated subject, but there are still some points of theoretical interest. The character changes and the absence of known physical cause suggest a psychological cause for the trouble, and some people describe this idiopathic epilepsy as psychogenic. There is often difficulty in diagnosing between hysteria and epilepsy, and this is complicated by the fact that an epileptic fit can be brought on by psychological causes. Prolonged observation may sometimes be necessary before the distinction can be made. I once asked a distinguished psychoanalyst if he had ever analysed a patient with epilepsy and he replied, "No, but I have analysed two that had been diagnosed as epilepsy and they turned out to be hysteria."

One recent discovery has found application in this disease and must be mentioned. When action takes place in some cells of the body there is a minute escape of electricity through the cell wall which can be detected by modern methods, and by taking advantage of this we have learnt a great deal about the sequence and nature of the heart's muscular contractions in health and disease. The activity of the cells of the brain can be likewise measured; many mental activities are shown to be associated with electrical changes, and in health a regular rhythm can be observed. In undoubted cases of epilepsy the rhythm is altered in a characteristic fashion, and this is obviously of use in diagnosis.

In the epilepsy described above it may be noted that interest has gradually shifted from the fit itself to the mental make-up of the man who suffers from it. In those cases of convulsions in which a physical cause is to be found there is naturally a shifting of interest again from the fit itself to the underlying morbid condition. As to this one can say that any condition capable of irritating the surface of the brain can produce a convulsion. Injury, inflammation, tumours, cysts or parasites, even some drugs, are among the recognized causes, and treatment must, of course, be directed in accordance with the physical diagnosis.

THE ORGANIC PSYCHOSES

The psychoses with no recognizable cause include the bulk

of patients in our mental hospitals, and there is room for much discussion as to whether we can hope ever to discover a material cause for them, discussion that often becomes more metaphysical than material. On the other hand, psychoses with an obvious physical cause easily outvie them in variety though not in numerical importance, except for general paralysis of the insane (often called G.P.I.) which accounts for about 10 per cent of the mental hospital population.

This has been recognized for over a century, but its syphilitic origin was not fully demonstrated till 1913, when the *treponema pallidum*, the organism that causes syphilis, was shown to be present. During life there is evidence of disease of the central nervous system, and gross disease of the brain and its coverings is found *post mortem*. Only about 2 per cent of the victims of syphilis suffer from G.P.I., and nothing is really known about why the disease should take this course in a few cases. G.P.I. generally follows an acquired infection, and develops on the average between the ages of thirty and fifty, though syphilis transmitted to the offspring can produce a juvenile form.

It begins with character changes, a loss of judgement and of response to social standards, which may be the first things to be noted by friends and relatives, the man himself having no realization of the alterations in his personality. Gradually all the mental faculties are diminished and, physical deterioration adding to the picture, the patient becomes entirely dependent upon nursing care. The patient may be depressed, but often there is a paradoxical sense of well-being, and delusions of a characteristic type occur. These involve grossly exaggerated ideas of superhuman strength or fantastic riches, and occasionally the first behaviour to mark the disorder is the embarking upon extravagant schemes. A story, that ought to be true, is told of a man setting out to sell a valuable estate and finding a purchaser for it at a very high price; then he was discovered to be a G.P.I. and the estate to be non-existent. The purchaser turned out to suffer from the same complaint and his money was imaginary, so, instead of the respective lawyers completing the transaction, the doctors were called in.

The outlook for the disease was formerly very bad, the end coming in from two to five years, for anti-syphilitic treatment had little or no effect. But it was noted that an attack of illness with a high temperature was often followed by amelioration of the disease, and, after some experimentation with other means of inducing pyrexia, the malaria treatment was instituted, and is now well established. A carefully selected strain of tertian malaria is used to infect the patient, and when it is judged expedient the resulting attacks of fever are easily brought to an end by the use of quinine. It is likely that the treatment acts by the rise of temperature killing the infecting organism and thus arresting the further progress of the disease; but nerve tissue cannot recover as other tissues in the body can, so that the damage already done to the brain is irremediable, and only when the damage is slight can a useful recovery be expected. In one large series of patients treated in this way over a period of five years, 25 per cent had been discharged from hospital, three-quarters of whom had returned to work; 34 per cent had died and the rest remained in hospital.

EPIDEMIC ENCEPHALITIS (SLEEPY SICKNESS)

This disease was recognized about 1918. It is an infection by a virus, which is a living substance that, unlike ordinary bacteria, can pass through a filter. The primary attack may be recognized when it occurs, or be diagnosed as influenza or other acute disorder, or missed entirely, and then the disorder is recognized only by the results. The physical aspect need not concern us, except so far as to note that it is a definite inflammation of the brain.

It receives its popular name because its onset is often marked by a state of stupor or lethargy, but from the beginning the disease presents an extraordinary variety of symptoms. When the initial stage is passed and the chronic condition is reached there becomes manifest a difference in the reactions of adults and children. Adults tend to apathy or depression, with interference with volition and apparent intellectual deterioration—one says apparent because it may depend upon the emotional state. Sometimes there is, however, a sense of well-being like that in G.P.I.

In children there comes about a change to behaviour

comprising every imaginable form of misdemeanour. Punishment has no effect and the handling of these children and adolescents has produced a social and even a legal problem. Some have found their way into mental hospitals, but the Mental Deficiency Act of 1927 contained provisions that would allow the inclusion of adolescents suffering from this disease and thus render unnecessary their being placed among adult patients.

In the treatment some drugs have a limited value and juvenile cases profit when placed under special care in a suitable institution, but when the chronic changes are established the final outlook is not good, though improvement does sometimes occur.

An important theoretical question arises in these juvenile cases. Here a definite brain disease is followed by serious behaviour disorders, which, even at their worst, differ only in degree from what may and do occur in troublesome and delinquent children who have never had the disease. Does the disease so stimulate the brain centres as to produce these symptoms? To agree to that we should have to conceive of a part of the brain that, when stimulated by disease, is capable of producing abusive language, violence, thieving, and what-not. It seems easier to picture the trouble as a loss of higher control that allows primitive impulses to express themselves. Something like that may be supposed to happen with the grandiose delusions of G.P.I., but we are still left guessing why that particular kind of delusion should come to the surface.

General paralysis of the insane and sleepy sickness comprise the bulk of the organic psychoses. A psychosis marked by confusion and physical weakness often follows severe infections or childbirth and needs prolonged nursing, but ends, as a rule, in recovery (the delirium of fevers, the nature of which often varies in correspondence with the kind of fever, is not classified as a psychosis). Old age has its well-known changes within wide limits of normality, but there is a senile psychosis in which a restless activity, often by night, with some degree of delusion or hallucination, makes extra care necessary. Alcohol can lead to mental disease with its own peculiar kind of phantasy-making, and the addiction to this and other drugs is a study in itself. I should, however, like to plead for a reconsideration of the emotion expressed in such words as "drug-fiend" and "morpho-maniac." There has been an unjustified working-up of this emotion, which probably started with an imaginative picture of an Oriental "opium den." My first acquaintance with opium smoking was half a century ago in Queensland, when the Chinese cook on a cattle station would have his opium brought up with the rest of the rations and carry on with his job happily and efficiently. In pre-revolutionary China one's boys smoked it and no one bothered, and local insurance companies would accept as a first-class risk a smoker who had settled down to a stabilized dose. Morphia addicts in this country, and alcoholics too, include psychopathic personalities and sufferers from nervous conditions who have found a false haven of refuge in the use of the drug. Among the morphine addicts, however, there are some who have reached their condition through the continued use of the drug for a reasonable cause, and could carry on with their regular dose, doing no harm to themselves or anyone else, but for the law. I have listened to bitter complaints from a lady who was in such a position, having acquired the habit during a long and painful illness. She had for long been on a constant dose, was now in good health, earning her own living, but, as she reiterated, was regarded as a criminal and an outcast. I believe that in this case the administrators of the law ultimately acted in the light of common sense, but the emotional condemnation remained. A doctor who, whilst suffering from severe nervous symptoms, acquired the morphia habit under the strain of active war service to which he should never have been subjected, succeeded in stabilizing his dose but dared not continue with it. He submitted himself to a course of drastic treatment that carried him over the distress of the deprivation period, and was then advised to take a long holiday. He came back from the holiday an alcoholic addict, and, though that addiction bore with it less of a moral stigma, the results were more disastrous for himself and his family. I am not an advocate of free access to morphia for everybody, but the moral condemnation that makes an Ishmael of every unfortunate drug addict could surely find a better object. I believe it plays a part in producing the scheming and deceit so often associated with addiction.

Among the organic psychoses is one with a curious history, pellagra. This was a terribly prevalent disease in some parts of the world (Italy and the Balkans particularly), with changes in the skin, intestinal symptoms, and signs of involvement of the actual nerves, up to 10 per cent of the sufferers showing mental symptoms. It was once ascribed to the use of diseased maize, but it is now known to be due to a dietetic deficiency, the excessive use of maize being associated with the lack of "protective" foods like milk, meat, and leguminous vegetables. It has occurred in mental hospitals in patients who were allowed to restrict their diet, and it occasionally crops up in people who live a secluded life and feed themselves wrongly. Prisoners of war in Japanese hands in the Far East suffered from it and from other hitherto unrecognized nutritional disorders with occasional mental symptoms.

A final word as to heredity in the psychoses. The study of heredity in these troubles is difficult because we are not dealing with clear-cut units. The possession of brown eyes, for example, is a unit, a man has them or has not, and their inheritance can be studied on Mendelian principles. Schizophrenia is not such a unit; it shades off into other disorders, and the "schizoid" make-up plays a dubious part when we come to study pedigrees. All the psychoses without known organic basis can occur in a family with no previous history of the incidence of the disorder. Yet there is certainly a hereditary factor, and marriage between two people with a family history of such disorders is not desirable.

By contrast there is one rather uncommon psychosis, Huntingdon's chorea, with an organic basis, which behaves as a unit and is directly inherited according to the rules of Mendelian transmission. It is very rarely seen without known inheritance.

CHAPTER VIII

LIE DETECTORS

Every now and again our interest in the wonderful is stimulated by news of a lie detector that, it is claimed, either compels a man to tell the truth or reveals when he is lying, and we think what wonderful people these psychologists are. No serious psychologist would make such a claim, which appeals much more to the mechanical-minded person, but since it is based upon work by psychologists it should be examined. It may refer to any one of several procedures.

The Word-Association Test

This has been in use for some forty years and was the subject of a comprehensive book by Jung in 1919. In the test the subject is invited to reply with the first word that comes to him in response to each of a series of "stimulus words" read out by the experimenter, who measures the time taken in each reply. Used frivolously it is little more than a parlour game, but with a calm and serious atmosphere useful results are obtained.

We can consider each word as a question, "What do you think of so-and-so?" and the experimenter has an unlimited choice of words whilst the victim never knows what is coming next. Standard lists are given in the books in which a hundred innocent-looking words have been chosen that are likely to touch emotional matters. Nearly everyone has had, or has, some emotional difficulty, some skeleton in the cupboard, and when this "complex" is stirred up by the stimulus word the victim makes an effort to retain his secret. But it fills his mind for the moment and if he uttered the first word that came he might reveal it; so he must thrust that, and others, aside and find a neutral word that will not betray him. Whilst he does this the stop-watch ticks on and if his usual reaction time is, let us say, three seconds, it may extend to six or eight on this item, or, if he is badly touched, he may maintain complete silence. To every word that affects his complex he will give a prolonged reaction time, and when the list is completed the experimenter has before him a record of the words that have emotional value for the victim.

What happens next is a matter for specific decision. If the test has been done for therapeutic reasons the two people concerned may now co-operate in trying to unravel the problem, for the result may point to some complex of which the patient is only dimly aware or which he has not yet had the courage to discuss. Used thus, it has an obvious relation to psycho-analysis and it has been used as an adjuvant to that process.

The procedure should not be undertaken lightly, for dis-concerting results might follow. In my early days I was in the house of Mr. A., a scientific man, where Mr. B., a friend of his possessed of a healthy scepticism, threw doubt upon the utility of the test and accepted my offer to submit himself to it. I had no prepared list and used such stimulus words as came into my head. At the fifth word the subject gave no reply and showed signs of perturbation, at which I remarked that something had hit him and we had better stop; we stopped, no one sought or offered any explanation, and only long after-ward did I learn of Mr. B's trouble and understand how my chance selection of a word had hit the mark. On another occa-sion I saw a colleague put a friend through a similar trial experiment. Nothing dramatic happened, but at the end of the test the operator remarked to the victim, "You are worrying about that son of yours," and had his surmise frankly admitted.

A well-known experiment with a psychology class is as follows:

Two students are taken aside by the demonstrator. A. is told something like this: "You threw a brick through a jeweller's window yesterday and grabbed an unset pearl. You cut your hand badly and dropped the pearl on the pavement. It rolled into the gutter and lay in the mud. You picked it up, making your hand muddy, and bolted down the street. People chased you and you left a trail of blood behind. You got away but are afraid of being found out. Now we shall put you through a word-association test and you must not give yourself away." The other student, B., knows nothing of the story and both are now put through the test before the class, who know the story and are invited to detect the imaginary criminal.

Scattered in the list are, let us suppose, the words brick, window, mud, pearl, blood, chase, guilt, policeman, in any order you please. The rest is easy. To B. these words have no significance and he replies without pause or confusion: to A. each one calls up the crime and he must hunt around for a response that will not reveal its application to himself; this takes time and each response stands out from the others by its lengthened reaction time.

The limitation of the test as a "lie detector ' is shown by this experiment. A sensitive person who knows that a particular crime is the subject of the test may react as if he were the criminal, and the only successful use of the test to detect a criminal, that I know in the literature, was in a school where thefts had occurred but were known only to the authorities and, of course, the thief. The subjects were told they were taking part in a scientific experiment and did not know its real object. Hence the thief had no idea that his reactions might give him away—but they did. Even then the result could hardly have been accepted as legal proof, but only served as a guide to further enquiry.

There are other uses of the test, such as to obtain indications as to the temperament of the subject or diagnostic indications about his mental state, but they do not concern us here.

The question arises how far this test will work in the presence not merely of a desire to conceal something but of an established dissociation of consciousness or a repression. In the case of the infantile repressions that can be uncovered by psychoanalysis the test has no value at all; I am satisfied, too, that in at least some war cases the dissociation of war experience from the main personality is so complete that appropriate stimulus words produce no effect. One might say that they are only effective when the subject becomes aware of their significance. The next procedure to be described is perhaps capable of a little deeper penetration.

THE PSYCHO-GALVANIC REFLEX

If an electric current is passed through the body it meets with a resistance that can be measured by a galvanometer, which casts a ray of light upon a graduated scale. Any change in the body's resistance will therefore be shown by a movement of the ray of light along the scale, and some forty years ago it was discovered that a sudden emotion caused the resistance to alter. Here, then, was an alternative to the word-association test, for it is obvious that words can rouse emotion and the emotion can then show itself by something independent of the volition of the subject. Not only words, of course, for a flash of light or a startling sound will produce a movement of the indicator.

All this seemed to promise useful results, but although many investigators have worked at it nothing much has come of it, perhaps because the reaction is so delicate that it measures too much. Like the word test, it could be used with disconcerting results, as when a sceptical nursing sister was placed in the circuit whilst a humorously malicious experimenter stood by and recited a list of masculine names till the ray of light gave a big swing and the victim demanded her release from the chair. In some war patients with extensive amnesia it was possible, by going through a list of place names with fighting associations, to learn from the indicator which names had emotional significance and thereby to tell with reasonable certainty where the man had fought. The sceptic who may still regard these amnesias as feigned would perhaps accept such a result as evidence of lying, and I know of no simple means of proving him wrong. The psychologist knows that the dissociated stream is outside the awareness of the patient, but is, like the unconscious, capable of perceiving on its own; therefore he finds no difficulty in picturing the dissociated stream as perceiving the significance of the stimulus word, then affecting bodily reactions by the emotion aroused and thus altering the electrical resistance—all this happening without the main personality being aware of it. The situation has its parallel often enough when the emotion arising from a dissociated stream produces a physical symptom like vomiting or palpitation, the origin of which is a mystery to the sufferer and can only be revealed to him by some sort of analytical procedure.

OTHER WAYS OF DETECTING EMOTION

Pulse, blood-pressure, and respiration, are all affected by emotion and therefore their measurement may indicate when an emotion is roused. If the stimulus to the emotion is known then we may gain knowledge about the victim, just as in the preceding tests. Rhazes, a mediæval Arabian physician, relates how a young woman suffered from an illness of anomalous nature and how, with his fingers upon her pulse, he murmured the name of a local Adonis and was rewarded by noting an immediate increase in the pulse rate. The patient was obviously not in a hurry to tell her doctor about her emotional troubles, but let us hope he used his deduction about those troubles to help her to recovery by the pleasantest route.

Not so simple as the method of Rhazes was a machine I saw advertised some years ago, when lie detection was booming. The victim was cased in apparatus that measured the three physiological factors mentioned above; in addition he was in the circuit of a psycho-galvanometer and thus fully prepared for a word-association test. I do not think the certainty of the result would be in proportion to the number of gadgets used.

THE USE OF DRUGS TO ELICIT THE TRUTH

All the methods described above demonstrate only that some reference is of emotional significance for the subject. If he is co-operative he may tell us all he can about the matter thus indicated, but apart from that our results are at best only deductions. A further step would be taken if we could find a reliable means of making a man tell us something he would rather conceal. Methods of reviving lost memories or of unifying dissociated streams of consciousness, described in previous chapters, serve the purpose of making the man tell something he has concealed *from himself*, and his co-operation is necessary. I have reason to believe, however, that a very serious and deliberate crime, the knowledge of which has been repressed and replaced by a hysterical symptom, can remain inaccessible to the psychological approach, including hypnosis and the word-association test, though the man gives apparently full co-operation. In this case there was the need for the man to conceal the truth not only from himself but from the outside world, and this sets it in a class by itself. It differed from those in which, under the stress of war, some offence against humanity had been committed that was repugnant to the man's own conscience but which he could reveal with or without hypnosis, because of his trust in the psychotherapist and the assurance of his understanding.

Alcohol is an ancient instrument to loosen the tongue, and many a man has revealed his true self when talkative in his cups, but it is unlikely that deep secrets are thus uncovered. It was a commonplace, in the days of simple inhalation anæsthesia with ether or chloroform, for the patient to pass through an excited and talkative stage in which tabooed words or scraps of revealing conversation might come from most unlikely-looking people, and it was a point of honour among doctors, students, and nurses, to be unaware of them. In 1925 Pierre Janet wrote that, "ether, chloroform, and ethyl chloride have been used to bring about hypnotic sleep with some interesting results." A few years ago scopolamine, a drug of the henbane group, received some press attention as a lie detector in the States. It produces a kind of delirium in which a man might let loose something. Just before the last war these various pointers led to the use of a synthetic drug, pentothal, to bring about a drowsy state in which the patient is still *en rapport* with the operator and can be led to recall memories and experience emotion in the same way as he had done at the hands of psychotherapists without the aid of drugs. The new method called for less experience on the part of the operator, certainly for less active co-operation on the part of the patient, and was probably time-saving. It received a good press and appeared as a new lie detector.

Its results are curiously parallel to those of the old method. Sometimes it fails; sometimes the patient denies the truth of what he has said, and he may or may not have an amnesia for it afterwards. The emotional reaction varies greatly and occasionally an operator will go back to the anæsthetic practice of an earlier generation and, carrying the patient to the excited and talkative stage of ether anæsthesia, take advantage of it to liberate emotion that the other drug has failed to loosen.

Those of the older generation who used the drugless method were acting only in the patient's interest and with his collaboration, and for them no other motive than the patient's good was conceivable. Indeed, to any medical man, whether psychologically minded or not, the idea involved in the phrase "lie detector" is repugnant and can never enter into the doctor-patient relationship even though the new method may call only for consent rather than for collaboration.

We may ask, however, how far the stories brought out in these various methods are reliable. In the old days it was freely declared that they were inventions, and a case described by Dr. Rivers in 1917 was a milestone inasmuch as a terrifying episode of infancy was recalled by means of a dream in adult life and the accuracy of the recall was confirmed by the man's parents. I once had the luck to revive a memory of a detailed telephone conversation, whilst in the room, listening, was the man who was at the other end of the telephone at the time of the real incident, and he confirmed the verbal accuracy of the reproduction. I have noted other examples of minute detail in the filling in of an amnesia, and have had no reason to doubt its accuracy even if the detail is less elaborate in the waking state.

In my account of mediumism, however, I tell how phantasy crept into the material produced by a war-time patient, who recognized its nature when questioned about it in full consciousness. It seemed to be a kind of dreaming by day—not quite the same as day-dreaming—and not of serious import.

It happens, though rarely, that a patient produces phantasy when in a hypnoidal or hypnotic state and believes the phantasy when awake to full consciousness. Now we are approaching the sphere of delusion and the outlook becomes more serious. I have met this phenomenon twice; in one case the phantasy was obviously absurd and could be regarded as having only psychological or diagnostic significance; in the other the story— enacted most dramatically—was so serious and was supported by such detail, intelligently and earnestly elaborated in ordinary conversation, that some action in regard to it seemed imperative. Fortunately it involved definite dates, and cautious enquiry of the patient's family satisfied me that on these dates the things related could not have happened.

When these possibilities of gross error are considered it is plain that whilst all these methods are useful for research and treatment yet to give them value as "lie detectors" is dubious. It is notable that the detector is always something mechanical, something to record on a machine or to inject with a syringe, and therefore appeals to the mechanically minded.

CHAPTER IX

THE PLACE OF PSYCHOPATHOLOGY IN HUMAN AFFAIRS

THERE have been many references to controversy in the preceding chapters, and most readers will find in this book something to repudiate or doubt. With a vital subject, still in active growth, this is to be expected, but the primary opposition to psychological and, more particularly, to psychoanalytical principles had an intensity almost without equal in the history of science. The significance of this opposition was hardly recognized at the time and is understandable now only when viewed in perspective.

Not so long ago man, with a few thousand years of civilization behind him, believed that this earth was the centre of all things, that sun, moon, and stars were rotating accessories whose function was to provide him with light, warmth, and entertainment. This geocentric pride was shocked when Copernicus declared that the apparently fixed earth did the rotating. The imprisonment and recantation of Galileo must have received the approval of all the right-thinking people of the day, but, finally, the now orthodox ideas about the motions of our earth relative to its immediate heavenly environment were accepted. We do not know how and by what stages the change took place but, to judge by later parallels, we must suppose there was no recantation of the older view. It is likely that the die-hards stopped talking in public before they finally succumbed.

Man still cherished the belief that he was the final product of a special act of creation, with woman as an afterthought, whilst the lower animals were created and ordained, like sun and moon in the earlier cosmogony, to serve his needs and pleasures. This anthropocentric pride made him react vigorously to Darwin's theory of evolution, by which he became subject to the same natural laws as were the humblest of his fellow creatures, with whom he now shared a common ancestry.

We are near enough to that controversy for some of the elders to remember that, near its final phase, evolution was admitted as probable but man himself was still to be excluded from relationship to the other mammals. Of one of my teachers, Arthur Keith, our hospital poet wrote in 1900—about forty years after the publication of *The Origin of Species* :

> "Far has he gone into Eastern climates,
> Taught man his place with the rest of the primates."

This shows that, whilst accepting the outcome as settled, we students recognized how recent was the final skirmish. The battle was over, but there was never any shouting. Opposition just ceased. I can remember that occasionally a fairly well-read person might express surprise or even incredulity when told that scientific men on the whole had accepted the doctrine of man's evolution, but gradually it had come about that nearly all interested people took the theory for granted.

In Keith's room hung a portrait of Thomas Huxley, who on a famous occasion was asked by a bishop whether he traced his descent from the ape on his father's side or his mother's, and later put on record, as a mnemonic for remembering the position of the mitral valve of the heart, the aphorism that a bishop was never in the right. I commend these stories to the notice of those who picture all Victorians as smug and complacent. Admittedly there was something like a belief that we had nearly reached the limits of knowledge of the natural world, and it was with mixed pride and humility that Huxley wrote:

> "The chessboard is the world; the pieces are the phenomena of the universe; the rules of the game are what we call the laws of nature. The player on the other side is hidden from us. We know that his play is always fair, just, and patient. But also we know to our cost that he never overlooks a mistake or makes the smallest allowance for ignorance."

By the end of the century we were coming to believe that the principle of the survival of the fittest had placed man, the only reasoning creature, well on the road to control his own destiny. Now, nearly half-way through the next, we are not so sure. We have knowledge outside the conception of the intellectual giants of the earlier generation. We have survived two World Wars and now envisage (in the true sense of that maltreated word) the risk of a third, with the possibility of its leading to the collapse of civilization. Man, who can control the atom, cannot control himself. What we must fear are no longer the laws of nature, except so far as man himself is a part of nature.

We can all realize that, without psychological help. Times were different when psychologists first shocked man by attributing to him instincts he had already postulated as marking the animal world, and an unconscious he had never suspected. They were slow to recognize the full significance of their own findings. This was, however, immediately clear to the direct heirs of nineteenth-century science, who cried aloud that psychoanalysis dethroned reason. Brought up in a school that regarded Huxley as the great man of his time (a view to which I still adhere) I was at one period bewildered to find the most unyielding opponents of the new psychological views among those whose upbringing was identical with my own.

Now, taking a historical view, we must believe that Huxley was, in spite of his scientific principles, a member of the herd like the rest of us, and that if he had lived long enough he would have opposed psychoanalysis.[1] As I showed in the first chapter, medical teaching, in the development of which Huxley had played a considerable part, excluded any psychological point of view. His acceptance of taboo is indicated in his textbook of physiology for the use of schools, in which reproduction is not mentioned, the only reference to a difference in the sexes being the statement that in the male there are characteristic changes in the larynx during growth. But I cannot believe that Freud's views about sex would have seriously alarmed our scientific forefathers. Principles much more fundamental were concerned. Physical laws were supposed to govern all the processes of life and when man had learned those laws he would be master of his own fate, for, unless insane or imbecile, he knew all that

[1] He died, aged seventy, in 1895, one year after Freud and Breuer published their paper on the therapeutic revival of memories, which was the starting point of psychoanalysis.

was happening in his own mind, what he was doing, and why he was doing it. To challenge these assumptions—all the more powerful because never plainly formulated—was to dethrone reason and challenge science itself. Thus, though the Church had been the most vigorous opponent of Darwinism, the most vigorous opposition to psychoanalysis came from scientists and medical men. Freud describes the void that formed around him after his first communications to his Viennese colleagues about psychoanalysis, and how, during years of isolation, he settled down "like Robinson" as comfortably as possible on his lonely island. Nearly twenty years passed before medical men in this country recognized the threat to their peace of mind. Quotations from leading medical journals will show the strength of their reaction:

"It [psychoanalysis] is now exposed, blown upon and discredited. It has been very skilfully advertised, and has been made very profitable, but its day is now past." (1916.)

"Is it known that psychoanalysts (some have been given commissions) are at their pernicious work in the lunacy wards of our great war hospitals?" (1917.)

When this reaction had worn itself out the lay press took up the theme, and some of the misrepresentations of psychoanalysis then put forth still linger. An early suggestion of its application to the study of crime stimulated one of our more serious weeklies to present a poetically-conceived psychoanalyst invoking "the spirit of slime" to aid the criminal.

Gradually there came about a change very like what took place in regard to the earlier controversy. Then, man's last defence was to exclude his species from the sphere of evolution. Now, the patient under analysis may have harboured irrational and infantile impulses; but the healthy man was different. "Neurotics"—especially in Vienna—might be influenced by an unconscious, but not he. He was still the master of his fate, the captain of his soul. This phase passed, and psychoanalysis became incorporated into psychological and psychiatric ideas, and even accepted by general medicine, to a degree that can be recognized only by a close scrutiny of current literature as compared with that of a few years ago. One now sees books and articles in which the authors use psychoanalytical language and conceptions so freely that they seem to think these had never been disputed. At the same time one must admit there are medical writers who achieve a remarkable success in avoiding recognition of psychological aspects of their subject matter.

I think it is correct to say there is now no overt opposition to psychoanalysis as such. Whatever exists is derived from the nineteenth-century attitude to psychology as a whole. It is still declared that science is exact, that it deals with what can be weighed or measured, put on a plate or under a microscope, whilst psychology, or psychoanalysis, is not science. There would be no need to pay attention to that assertion if it bore the corollary that science should mind its own business; but it is often used to justify a denial of psychological facts. I prefer to define science as the unprejudiced search for truth, and to regard *The Origin of Species* and *The Interpretation of Dreams* as examples of the application of scientific method.

It is noteworthy that man's reaction against the theory of the unconscious exceeded both in duration and intensity that against Darwinism, and this difference measures its importance to his outlook upon himself and the world. He feared it as shaking his trust in himself and his institutions; and he was right.

In Chapter V of this book we saw how for centuries we had accepted without question the sex taboo as part of a normal and healthy society. In a footnote it was suggested that in the world to-day the emotional, irrational, and authoritative appeal, as manifested in the sex taboo, triumphs over the logical and understandable, and that the subservience of Germans to Hitler offered an example of that triumph. That was speculative. Now in *The Listener*, of June 5th, Professor Henry Dicks describes the results of his psychological study of German prisoners of war,[1] which provides ample evidence of the way in which the Nazi disease "is rooted so deeply in the

[1] Note, as a practical matter, the difference between a *psychological study* and a *psychoanalysis*. In one variety of the former the subject is encouraged to talk freely about himself and his views on life, the success of this method demanding specialized experience and technique. He is not expected to say or learn anything about his own unconscious processes,

whole structure of family and other inter-personal relationships, in the authoritarian way of education aud institutions." The sex taboo falls into place in the structure thus defined, and force is added to the questions of Professor Dicks—"Can anyone really claim that the other nations, ourselves included, are free from some of the undesirable features of the German character? Can humanity really, in this atomic age, say, 'It will not happen again?'"

We can now plot out the expanding field of modern psychopathology. First it was discovered that a psychoneurosis was a reaction, with unconscious origins, called forth by a family situation; then that the family situation itself had its unconscious origins. This was sometimes expressed in two aphorisms, rarely put in black and white; namely, that if a child was brought for treatment the parent needed it, and if one spouse came for treatment the other partner needed it. Next, the principle expressed in these aphorisms was applied to delinquency, serious crime, and sexual perversions, which called for the study of the unconscious foundations of the prejudices and *mores* of society itself.

War, like these other disadvantageous phenomena, is a matter of human behaviour. If it cannot be avoided man will go under, and the more successfully he investigates nuclear physics the sooner he will go.

Henry Dicks's psychological study of German prisoners of war was officially a recognition that something useful was expected from the examination of the Nazi corpse. What emerged is that every nation's culture and institutions, its worship of heroes and its fear of bogey-men, its slogans and witchwords, call for understanding and must be psychologically studied without reservation if we are to have any hope of averting war.

Shaw, who is now old enough for his opinions to be treated

though the investigator may, if so inclined, make deductions guided by psychoanalytical knowledge. The whole process occupies a few hours at most.

In a psychoanalysis the aim is that the subject should reach a knowledge of his own unconscious processes, which then becomes a fact of observation and not a deduction. The process needs a different technique and may last up to several hundred hours.

with respect, made O'Flaherty, V.C., say, "You'll never have a quiet world till you knock the patriotism out of the human race." To this I would add that we shall never get honest thinking so long as we teach our young to call a water-closet a lavatory; and whoever is shocked by these sentiments will understand what I mean above by *studied without reservation*.

To cite Professor Dicks again: "Are nuclear physicists really the only people who are going to be endowed with great funds for research? Or does it not matter about the mentality of the people who will handle the forces the physicists are placing at their disposal?" As one who has been through the controversial mill I can assure the reader that the public expression of such ideas by a psychologist of standing would have been impossible a few years ago, and is itself evidence of wonderful progress. Psychopathology has no ready-made solution of the problems that face us. It can, however, in co-operation with such allied sciences as anthropology and sociology, point out the road to be followed in the unprejudiced search for truth, with the hope that it may eventually lead to the enthronement of reason and make man the master of his fate.

BOOKS SUITABLE FOR NON-MEDICAL READERS

ALLEN, CLIFFORD. *Modern Discoveries in Medical Psychology.* MacMillan, 1937. 8s. 6d. Contains a chapter each on Jung and Adler.

BUTLER, SAMUEL. *The Way of All Flesh.* A well-known study of the results of a misguided upbringing.

BURT, CYRIL. *The Young Delinquent.* Univ. of London Press. 4th ed., 1945, 21s.
——. *The Backward Child.* As above. 2nd ed., 1946, 25s.
——. *How the Mind Works.* Broadcast talks by Cyril Burt, Ernest Jones, Emanuel Miller and William Moodie. Edited by Cyril Burt. Allen and Unwin, 3rd ed., 1945. Each author deals with his own aspect of the subject.

ELLIS, HAVELOCK. *Psychology of Sex.* Heinemann. 10th impression, 1946, 15s. A comprehensive survey.

FLUGEL, J. C. *The Psycho-Analytic Study of the Family.* Hogarth Press, 7th ed., 1947. 10s. 6d.

FREUD, SIGMUND. *An Autobiographical Study.* Hogarth Press. 2nd ed., 1946, 6s. A personal story of the development of his ideas.

GESELL, ARNOLD. *How a Baby Grows.* A pictorial study of emotional development up to the age of five. Hamish Hamilton Med. Books, 1946, 10s. 6d.

GLOVER, E., *War, Sadism and Pacifism.* Allen and Unwin, 1947, 9s. 6d. A study by a well-known psychoanalyst.

HARDING, D. W. *The Impulse to Dominate.* Allen and Unwin, 1941, 7s. 6d. A study of the social implications of war and its probable psychological origins.

HART, BERNARD. *The Psychology of Insanity.* Camb. Univ. Press, 1912; last reprint 1946, 3s. 6d.

ISAACS, SUSAN. *Social Development in Young Children.* Routledge and Sons, 1945, 18s. A detailed account of child development as observed by a psychoanalyst.

READ, H. *Education Through Art*. Faber and Faber, 1946, 25s. A psychological study of the significance of art.

REES, J. R. *The Shaping of Psychiatry by War*. W. W. Norton; New York, 1945, $2.50. Lectures given in America by the brigadier responsible for organizing our army psychiatry. Shows the influence it may be expected to have on psychiatry in civil life.

SMITH, MAY. *An Introduction to Industrial Psychology*. Cassel, 1943, 7s. 6d. Shows, *inter alia*, the importance of temperament in industry.

WINTERTON, P. *Mending Minds*. Peter Davies, 1938. 8s. 6d. An able account of mental hospital work, by a professional journalist.

SOME DEFINITIONS

AFFECT. A word used by psychologists rather in the sense of the Shakespearean *affection* in

> . . . affection,
> Mistress of passion, sways it to the mood
> Of what it likes or loathes.

It signifies a directive force bearing with it a positive or negative emotion. Hence mania and melancholia are called *affective* disorders.

ANXIETY. As used in the diagnostic phrase *anxiety state* this word refers to pathological anxiety not wholly or chiefly accountable to current stress; for that we can use the more homely word *worry*.

COMPLEX. A collection of unconscious ideas held together by a particular emotional quality. The phrase *inferiority complex* is a misuse of the word; the speaker generally refers to something fully conscious and should say inferiority *feeling*, or, if he wishes to be technical, *sentiment*.

DEMENTIA. The loss of mental faculties once present. If they have never been present the condition is *amentia*.

NEUROSIS. A word with a long and varied history. Is now used in two different senses: (1) to indicate a bodily symptom, like a "cardiac neurosis," in which an organ is affected through interference with its nerve control, and (2) any mental disorder not belonging to the group *psychosis* (which see).

The second usage, though of recent growth, arose from the traditional mechanistic assumption described in Chapter I. It seems well established, but both groups are really psychoses and in the interests of scientific accuracy it would be well to recognize that fact. Meanwhile we must accept neurosis in place of the old "neurasthenia" as a rubbish heap made up of practically all the psychological disorders that are not insanities. (*See* Psychoneurosis.)

NEURO-PSYCHIATRIST. Indicates a medical man who has had special training in neurology as well as psychiatry. In this country it appears to be used also as a token of belief in the physiological cause of all psychological disorders. Many psychiatrists avoid it.

PSYCHIATRIST. A physician who treats diseases of the mind. First used to indicate one who cared for insane people, it now includes all medical men engaged in the treatment or handling of psychoses, psychoneuroses, childhood problems, delinquency, and such-like. Some medical psychoanalysts still prefer to be classed apart from psychiatrists.

PSYCHOANALYST. Should be confined to one trained in the principles and practice of psychoanalysis as they have developed from the teachings of Freud. Some non-medical psychoanalysts are recognized as well-trained and competent, and it is probable that such people will be legitimately employed in the future under medical supervision.

PSYCHOGENIC. Produced by mental processes, intellectual or emotional, unconscious or conscious. May be applied to a specific symptom or a general state.

PSYCHOLOGIST. One, medical or not, who is trained in the study of the mind. The title covers a wide range, from the university professor to the industrial or educational psychologist, and it is desirable that it should be limited to those having some hallmark of training such as a degree or diploma in the subject.

PSYCHONEUROSIS. A clumsy word, preferable to neurosis, used to indicate what are popularly called "nervous" disorders. (*See* Neurosis.)

PSYCHOPATHOLOGY. The study of the mental processes underlying a disorder.

PSYCHOTHERAPIST. Till recently this indicated a medical man who treated the psychoneuroses, as distinct from the psychiatrist, who treated psychoses or insanities. This distinction is now practically gone.

PSYCHOSIS. Disorder of the mind. Is usually confined to a group of disorders which typically, but not always, lead to social maladjustment necessitating institutional care. (*See* Neurosis.)

INDEX

(f) denotes footnote.

For Product Safety Concerns and Information please contact our EU
representative GPSR@taylorandfrancis.com
Taylor & Francis Verlag GmbH, Kaufingerstraße 24, 80331 München, Germany